In a Latke Trouble

To Lucas –
I hope you like this
book "A Latke!"
♡,
Dori Weinstein
:)

Books in the
YaYa & YoYo Series

Praise for *In a Latke Trouble* (YaYa & YoYo, Book 4)

"*In a Latke Trouble* is charming, sweet, funny, and has a great message without being didactic. Weinstein has such a sure hand for storytelling, a good grasp of the age group, and I love all the humor. YaYa and YoYo are fallible yet have good hearts (*such* good hearts). YaYa and YoYo are totally real to me, and it's always a pleasure to spend time in their world. Dori Weinstein has done it again. I love this book!"

Jennifer Wilson
Author of *Someday We'll Find It*

"This multicultural Hebrew School mash-up invites readers on a journey from the ancient Holy Temple in Jerusalem to the world of a fifth-grade friend group, with surprising connections and lessons to be learned. *In a Latke Trouble* shines a light on essential Hanukkah themes: the dangers of group conformity and the value of personal bravery. Friends learn to deal with peer pressure, make good choices, and rededicate themselves toward making this world a better place. Dori Weinstein's fourth installment of YaYa & YoYo will brighten readers' minds and inspire their souls!"

Rabbi Menachem Creditor
Scholar in Residence, UJA-Federation of New York
Author of *A Rabbi's Heart*

"YaYa and YoYo are back with a whole new set of adventures and hijinx, this time leading up to the holiday of Hanukkah. With a wider cast that is representative of contemporary schools, Weinstein once again proves that she has her ear to the ground when it comes to kids, deftly weaving in values and morals without tipping her hand and bogging down the story. A highly recommended fun read for kids and parents alike, with plenty to laugh about, think about, and discuss!"

Natalie Blitt
Author of *The Truth About Leaving*;
The Distance From A to Z;
Carols and Crushes; and *Snow One Like You*

"*In a Latke Trouble* is a true gem! I feel like I know YaYa and YoYo personally. They are witty, courageous, and always strive to be the best versions of themselves. I love how Weinstein showcases the beauty and nuance found in contemporary Jewish life. She simultaneously tells a compelling story while also conveying the deeper meaning of Hanukkah. Readers will delight in this charming holiday tale!"

Elana Rubinstein
Author of the Saralee Siegel series

"Dori Weinstein does it yet again. I've long searched for age-appropriate, engaging, Jewish chapter books for my own children. The YaYa and YoYo series is the only one that seems to "age up" with the children. This new volume especially provides just enough intrigue and insight to keep the young reader not only engaged but wanting more. And it's a perfect Hanukkah gift to boot!"

Rabbi Avi S. Olitzky
Beth El Synagogue, St. Louis Park, Minnesota
Contributor, *Text Messages: A Torah Commentary for Teens*

In a Latke Trouble

Dori Weinstein

Five Flames Press

Copyright © 2021 by Dori Weinstein

YaYa & YoYo: In a Latke Trouble
First edition—September 2021
Five Flames Press

www.yayayoyo.com

Cover illustration by © Ann D. Koffsky
Cover graphics by Ward Barnett
Editor: Leslie Martin

ISBN-13: 978-0-9890193-3-0

In a Latke Trouble is being released ten years after the very first YaYa & YoYo book, *Sliding into the New Year*, was published. This book is dedicated to all the kids who have become "friends" with Ellie and Joel Silver over the past decade, as well as to all the future YaYa & YoYo fans who have not met them yet, but are about to.

And, as always, this book is dedicated to Gary, Ari, Ilana, and Eitan. My world. You make the magic happen.

Contents

1

Pick a Card, Any Card

I thought my head was going to explode.

I stood in front of my sister with a handful of cards fanned out in front of her, at eye level.

"Just pick one! Literally, any card. Just. Pick. One!" I said, trying to stay calm. She stared at the cards from her seat at the kitchen table, her face all scrunched up reminding me of a shriveled potato.

We'd been at this for at least six minutes.

"Come on!" It felt like my patience was draining right out of my body and leaking all over the floor. Good thing that couldn't really happen because our dog, LuLu, would be right there to lick it all up—she'll lick anything she sees in front of her.

"I can't decide," Ellie said, sounding tormented. "What if I choose the wrong one?" She wrapped a clump of her long, brownish-blonde hair around her finger, then let it go, and repeated this over and over while she concentrated on the cards.

"You're killing me here, YaYa," I moaned. "There's no right or wrong card. Just pick one and then I'll be able to show you the trick."

My twin sister, Ellie, otherwise known as YaYa in our family, tapped her chin with the hand that wasn't twirling her hair. "Ummm..." she said, studying the cards as if her life depended on it. Good thing it was a Sunday afternoon and we didn't have anywhere to go.

"It's just a dumb magic trick!" I said, raising my voice in frustration. Then I actually hollered.

"Pick a card already!"

"Don't rush me, YoYo!" she hollered back. "I'm working on it!" She squinted, her eyes darting from one card to the next, as if choosing the wrong one would start a nuclear war with a foreign country.

"Rush you? At the pace you're going, we'll be graduating from college by the time you finally pick a card." I rolled my eyes and finally said in a huff, "I'm about to walk away, YaYa."

"Okay, okay, okay!" She grabbed my arm. "Stay! Stay! Okay, I'll pick. I choose...this one," she said, and pulled a card from the deck. "No, wait, this one." She tucked the first one back in and plucked out another.

"Great," I said, without my usual over-the-top enthusiasm. Being a magician is all about showmanship and keeping people entertained, but it took her so long to pick a card that even I, the magician, lost interest. Too bad she was my only audience at the moment. Since Ellie and I are twins, we end up spending a lot of time together, sometimes by choice and sometimes just because that's the way things work out. We're both in fifth grade at Alexander Martin Elementary school, and we both go to Camp Shemesh in the summer. Like most other siblings, sometimes we get along and sometimes we annoy the heck out of each other. This was one of those times.

Now and then she bugs me on purpose. For instance, when she treats me like I'm her baby brother. She used to even call me her "Little Bro" all the time. I mean, come on, we're twins! Born only thirteen minutes apart! Not only that, since she was born five minutes *before* midnight on October 8th and I didn't come out until eight minutes *after* midnight the next day, she claims that she's a *whole day* older than me. It's true, we have different birthdays, and one could argue that she's technically a day older. However, I always point out that because we're Jewish, we should go by the Hebrew calendar, where a day begins at sundown. Looking at it that way, we were actually born on the exact same day. She prefers to ignore that fact.

"Okay, YoYo, dazzle me!" she said. "Are you going to guess which card I picked?"

I rolled my eyes at her again. She always gets so excited about things. I do too, I guess, but definitely not about the same things. We're pretty different in a lot of ways. All you'd need to do is look in our bedrooms to see. Mine is neat, organized, and orderly, with useful things hanging on the walls like a poster of the solar system and a world map. Her room looks like a bunch of wild goats recently invaded and went digging around for food, which they'd probably find in there. She has a life-size poster of her music idol, Corey McDonald, and a jumble of other papers, pictures, and magazine cut-outs randomly taped up around the room. It feels like a volcano barfed up assorted clutter and it all stuck to the walls wherever it landed.

One thing we do have in common is our family nicknames. Ellie's Hebrew name is *Yael*. My name in English is Joel, and in Hebrew it's *Yoel*. Yep, that's right, Yael and Yoel. When I was learning how to talk, I tried to say our Hebrew names but they came out all wrong. Instead of Yael and Yoel, I said YaYa and YoYo. To this day, that's what everyone in our family calls us. Our older brother Jeremy was about three when this all went down, and didn't want to be left out. He insisted that everyone in the family call him YerYer since his

Hebrew name is *Yeremiyahu*. Our parents thought YerYer sounded weird, so they talked him out of it and convinced him to go by JayJay instead. Now he mostly goes by Jay, especially with his friends. In our house, it's not unusual to hear us each being called by our English name, Hebrew name, and nickname, sometimes even all within the same sentence.

"Are you going to guess which card I picked?" she repeated, even more excited than the last time.

"No," I answered flatly. I paused and waited for her reaction—and there it was, as expected: utter confusion and disappointment. But before she could say anything, I continued.

"I'm not going to *guess*. I *know*." Then I half-heartedly shuffled the cards and pulled out the six of diamonds. (It's possible that I may have even yawned.) "Is this your card?"

Ellie gasped as if I had presented her with a wad of hundred dollar bills. "No way! How'd you do that?" she cried out. "Do it again! Let me pick another card! Tell me how you did it!"

I've only recently started messing around with card tricks, and magic tricks in general. Making people laugh and surprising them is my favorite thing to do, which is why I'm also into comedy and telling jokes. I used to play a lot of pranks on people too. But I realized right around *Rosh Hashanah*, the Jewish new year, as I considered ways to do better and improve myself, that playing tricks on other people can be kind of mean. I kept at it for a while but started to feel bad about making my friends and family members look and feel foolish. I definitely don't want to be *that* guy, so I decided to find other ways to surprise and trick people. (I still love a good whoopie-cushion placement at just the right time, or putting googly eyes on every container in the fridge so when you open the door it looks like everything's looking at you—that's one of my favorites.)

I came across some old David Copperfield videos and now I'm hooked! He's an incredible, famous magician and illusionist. I could watch him perform all day long. In addition to magic, I've been trying my hand at juggling. My favorite thing of all, though, is when I can stump people with a good math trick. I've always loved math and science, and I've recently come to realize that I can sometimes astonish people just by using science facts, math, and logic.

Ellie continued her pleading, "Please show me how you did the trick! I can't believe you found my card so easily!"

"You know I'm not going to tell you, so you may as well stop asking already," I replied. Under normal circumstances, I love getting reactions like hers when I successfully pull off a trick, but she kind of killed it for me by taking so long. "Maybe I'll do it again later." It's good to keep your audience wanting more.

"Do what again later?" Jeremy asked, slinking over to the fridge and poking his head in, demonstrating that he didn't actually care about whatever it was that we were discussing. "Oh, man! Are we out of yogurt?" he complained. "I really wanted some."

"I don't know," I answered. "But there's, like, a million jars of Mom's homemade applesauce in there."

As if she had supersonic hearing, Mom came swooping into the kitchen and sang out, "No! Don't eat the applesauce, Jay! We need that for the *latkes* for *Hanukkah*."

Latkes are delicious fried potato pancakes that we

eat on the Jewish holiday of Hanukkah. Dad is the master chef and baker in our kitchen, but Mom has a few things that she really loves making, and this is one of her specialties. Every year she gets so excited when it's almost Hanukkah that she starts preparing applesauce to put on the latkes way sooner than we need it. And every year when she realizes that she's overdone it, we end up eating applesauce at almost every meal for a week or two before we even get to the latkes. Seriously, this happens every single year. It has become a Silver family tradition. At this point she was still in her we-won't-have-enough-applesauce-for-Hanukkah-if-you-eat-it-now phase. Next comes the oh-my-goodness-we-have-so-much-applesauce-in-here-you-need-to-eat-some-before-it-goes-bad phase.

I knew that we were on the verge of switching from Phase One to Phase Two, but apparently we weren't there yet because Mom deftly removed a cup of yogurt from behind a container of sour cream and handed it to Jeremy.

"Awesome! Thanks, Mom," Jeremy said, pulling the foil top off and licking it like a horse drinking out of a trough. He gulped the yogurt directly from the cup, not bothering to get a spoon. When he did this, he made a disgusting slurping sound that almost made me gag.

Jeremy's in seventh grade. He's only two months away from turning thirteen, and he gets grosser and grosser by the minute. His *bar mitzvah* is going to be in February, and supposedly—at least according to Jewish tradition—that's when he'll become a "man." Interestingly, the closer he gets to being a "man," the more immature he acts. Jeremy acting like a Jewish adult would probably be the most incredible magic trick of all. It's weird. Ellie and I are less than two years younger, but sometimes it feels like we are worlds apart.

The doorbell rang. LuLu, who had been fast asleep and snoring softly in her little dog bed in the kitchen, sprang to life. Her long white tail began to wag as fast as a hummingbird's wings. She bounced excitedly. Her little legs, which are brown half-way down and then white—like she's wearing boots—scurried across the kitchen floor to the front door, and her brown ears flopped up and down as she ran. She yipped and yapped at top volume. Not that I can speak in Dog, but loosely translated this means, "Someone's here! Open the door! This is the best moment in my life!" She reacts this way every single time there's a knock on the door or the doorbell rings.

"I'll get it," Mom said. "Are we expecting anyone?"

"I'm not," I answered.

"Me neither," said YaYa.

"Nope," Jeremy added.

Mom walked out of the kitchen to go see who it was. We were all curious. It's rare that one of our friends comes over without calling first. We figured it was most likely going to be someone with a clipboard asking for signatures for one cause or another, or maybe someone selling something. We left it to our mother to deal with the bell-ringer. Jeremy went back to his yogurt slurping, and Ellie continued begging me to do another trick.

Then we heard Mom say, "What a nice surprise!"

We all looked at one another, wondering who it could be. Mom wouldn't be *that* happy to see a random salesperson at our doorstep. Jeremy put down the yogurt cup and I left my deck of cards on the table, as all three of us went to see who was at the door.

2

Don't Call Me Aardvark!

H i, Mrs. Silver," a kid my age and my height said from the front stoop. "Is Joel home?" Even with a knit hat on his head, a scarf covering his nose, mouth, and chin, and his glasses fogged up from the cold, I'd know my best friend, Ari Wolff, anywhere.

I was shocked. Ari never comes over unannounced, even though he knows that he's always welcome and doesn't need an invitation since he's practically a part of our family. On the other hand, Ari's parents are very formal and fancy. When I go to his house, I always call his mom Dr. Packter and his dad Dr. Wolff. Unlike the Wolff-Pack family, as I like to call them, the Silver family could not possibly be any more laid back.

"Come in, come in," Mom said, "and for the eighteen-millionth time, Ari, please call me Debbie!" This same conversation has been going on for years. Ari always calls my parents Mr. and Mrs. Silver, and my parents always remind him to call them by their first names. It's almost like a ritual by now, like how we sing "The Star Spangled Banner" at the start of a baseball game, or how I make my bed as soon as I get out of it in the morning. Or how my sister doesn't.

"Thanks, Debbie," Ari said, mumbling her name uncomfortably like it hurt the inside of his mouth. I honestly don't think I've ever actually heard him say my parents' first names before. He usually mumbles something and quickly changes the subject. He turned around to give a thumbs-up to his parents who were waiting in their car, to let them know we were home and it was okay to hang out. Jeremy quickly exited the scene, realizing that our visitor wasn't here to see him. Ellie stuck around.

Before stepping inside, Ari stomped his feet on the doormat. A few snowflakes were coming down and his boots were wet. I'd been hoping for a huge snowstorm so I could go sledding or play in the snow. It always feels like such a waste when it snows like this. What's the point if you can't have a snowball fight, build a snow fort, or best yet, get a day off of school? Every little snowflake that floated through the air melted as soon as it hit the ground. It had been flurrying in the morning when we left our Sunday morning religious school class, which we call Shul School. (*Shul* is the Yiddish word for synagogue. Yiddish is an old Jewish language that's a mash-up of Hebrew and German.) Judging by Ari's boots, there'd be no snow day for us. He stepped into the foyer and slipped his feet out of his boots.

LuLu was so excited. She spun around in circles for a while and then went back and forth, jumping on Ari's legs, licking his hand, and sniffing the inside of his boots. Then she started the whole routine all over again. She performs this sort of choreography every single time someone shows up at the door, no matter who it is.

Ari removed the hat from his head, which made his stick-straight black hair stand up for a few seconds from the static electricity. He almost looked like he was floating through space thanks to his anti-gravity hair.

"Hey, Shmari! What's up?" I said. Everyone, except for LuLu, looked at me strangely. (LuLu was too busy finishing her "We have a visitor!" dance, which she wrapped up with one final lick of Ari's hand before trotting back to the kitchen to resume her nap.)

"Shmari?" Mom repeated with a puzzled look on her face.

Calling Ari "Shmari" was something new I'd been trying out. Some of my best buddies at school and I decided that we wanted to start a club. We didn't know what kind of club, but everyone in the group who wanted to could be in charge of something. Our friend Brady was going to be the leader since he brought up the idea in the first place. I volunteered to be in charge of making up nicknames for everyone. I'd been trying out different names on Ari but none had stuck yet. So far, "Ar-plane" and "Sa-fAri" were absolutely rejected. Earlier in the week when I tried suggesting "Tooth-fAri," he looked at me like I had started speaking in LuLu's language. "What are you trying to say to me?" he asked with a confused look.

"Tooth-fAri, you know, like the tooth fairy."

"Uh, no. No, no, and no," he said. I couldn't tell if he was insulted or kidding around, but it was clear that the answer was no. I had to keep trying, and knew I'd be able to tell if I hit the right one if he smiled or laughed when he heard it.

"Hey," he greeted me back without using my own new nickname, Coppy. I can't say I wasn't disappointed that he chose to skip it. I came up with Coppy because of my David Copperfield obsession, and how I've been trying to figure out how he does his amazing magic tricks. I'm not planning to attempt tricks as enormous as his, like the time he made the Statue of Liberty disappear, but I wouldn't mind learning a thing or two from him.

Ari ignored being called "Shmari" and said, "My parents are going shopping, and I really didn't want to go with them. I was hoping I could hang out with you for a little while." His parents like to do everything together "as a family," even boring chores like buying groceries or getting gas in the car. I don't get it. But anyway, Ari is an only child, and so he often gets roped into these outings because his parents don't want to leave him home alone. They seem to think these are fun activities, but Ari likes to squirm his way out of them whenever possible. The Silver home is always his escape plan.

"You know you're always welcome here," Mom said. Then she added while winking at me, "Shmari."

Ari shook his head at me as if to say, *I'm gonna get you for this!*

"You can do your card trick for him," Ellie exclaimed. "Now you have another audience member!"

"Yeah, maybe in a little while," I said. "But for now, we're going up to my room. Okay, Aardvark?" Ari shook his head violently at me.

"Absolutely not!" he said, looking like he'd just tasted some spoiled guacamole.

"Absolutely not, what?" I asked, confused. "You absolutely don't want to go upstairs or you absolutely don't like that nickname?" I really wasn't sure.

"Do *not* call me Aardvark!"

"Okay, okay," I said. "Sheesh! I was just trying to come up with something that starts out like your name with the 'Ar' sound. Why don't you come up with a new nickname then, since you don't like any of my ideas?"

"I never even said I wanted a nickname! What's the deal with that anyway?" he asked.

"I don't know," I replied with a shrug, "I thought it would be fun for all our buddies in the club to have nicknames. Kind of like a sports team. You know, like Pee Wee or Big Papi."

"What's the story with this club anyway?" Ari asked.

I shrugged again. "All I know is that Brady wants to start the club, and he said something about wanting to call us the Bravey Cats."

"What's a Bravey Cat? Are you sure he didn't say Brady Cats?" Ari asked with a furrowed brow.

"Yeah, I'm sure. And as for what it is, I have absolutely no idea. Come on, let's go upstairs. Maybe we can call him and find out more. What do you say...Archibald?"

Ari scowled. I kept trying.

"Arnold? Arthur?" I could see the smallest hint of a smile creeping up on his face. His sense of humor is almost identical to mine, so I knew he wouldn't be mad. Sooner or later I was bound to say something he thought was funny.

"Ugh! Let's go up and call Brady already!" Ari pointed up the staircase.

"Armadillo? Arkansas?" I kept throwing out names and random words, waiting to see when I'd hit the jackpot. "No wait! I've got it!" I said. "How about George Arshington?"

Ari stood there with his arms folded across his chest, shaking his head, saying, "No, no, no, no!" nonstop. I could tell he was trying hard to keep a straight face.

Jeremy strolled over to us, snacking on a handful of

grapes. "You're still choosing a nickname? Holy moley! You've been at it for over a week already. You are the worst at this!" He roared with laughter in the foyer. "Seriously. The worst!"

"Ooh!" I jumped up and down. "I just thought of the perfect name!" I made eye contact with everyone, doing my best showman's job of building suspense. My audience watched the nickname drama unfold like it was a movie. All we needed was a big bucket of popcorn. No one budged. "Wanna hear it?"

"Yes!" Ellie said.

"I think this one's the winner. It's awesome!" I said.

"Come on, already!" Ellie squeaked.

I took a deep, dramatic breath, waited another moment, and finally, after building up the suspense, announced, "Arlington National Cemetery."

"That's awful!" Mom said.

"You're kidding, right?" Ellie asked.

Ari stared at me, scrunching up his face, making him look both confused and furious. He couldn't hold back any longer and laughed straight from his gut. Got him!

"Arlington National Cemetery it is!" I hooted. "That's not the one I would have predicted you'd like, but if you think it's good, let's go with it."

Ari stopped laughing like a car screeching to a halt. His eyes got big and wide, and he gave me such a death stare that I felt a chill run through my body.

"No! Wait! You *cannot* call me Arlington National Cemetery!" he bellowed. Everyone in my family gaped at him. His face turned a bright shade of flamingo-pink and I wasn't sure if he was embarrassed or angry. Then he burst out laughing again, as did everyone else in the room.

"Well, obviously, we wouldn't call you Arlington National Cemetery, it's too long. Maybe we should just go with Cemetery," I said between laughs.

"Cemet-ARI!" Ellie chimed in.

"This is not happening!" Ari shouted, looking up to the ceiling. "Ugh! Maybe I should have gone shopping with my parents!" He could barely get the words out between giggles.

"How about Archie?" Mom suggested. I thought it was hilarious that now my family was getting involved.

Ari threw his hands up in the air and said, "Sure, Archie, whatever. I give up! Just don't call me Aardvark! And absolutely do NOT call me Arlington National Cemetery!"

"Oh, come on, Arlene, we were never actually going to call you Arlington National Cemetery. That wouldn't make any sense. You're not really a cemetery," I said, trying to keep a straight face.

"I'm also not an aardvark! And you can forget about Arlene. That's not happening!" he said between gasps. We were laughing so hard that the tears flowed down our cheeks. I love laughing so hard that it makes my stomach hurt. It's totally worth the pain.

After we calmed down and were able to breathe normally again, I said, "Okay, Armpit. Let's go."

Ari laughed so hard it almost sounded like he was weeping. The two of us, bent over with laughter, held our stomachs as we attempted to climb the steps to go to my room.

And *that* is why we're best friends.

3

What's a Bravey Cat?

Ari and I got permission to use my Mom's cell phone. We put Brady on speaker so the three of us could talk together.

"Hi, Brainy, it's Joel calling. Ari's here too," I said, feeling a little giggle come up just by using Brady's nickname. Brady's the guy at school who always comes up with schemes and plans. Back when I was doing practical jokes all the time, Brady was my very willing partner in crime, and came up with some of the most hysterical ideas.

"Did you just call me Brainy?" he asked. The funny thing is that Brady has allergies and often sounds like his nose is all stuffed up, so saying Brainy sounds kind of like how he pronounces his name normally.

"Yeah, that's your new club nickname," I informed him. "You like it?"

"Yeah, it's like my name but with an N instead of the D," he said, stating the obvious. "That's funny. What's your new nickname?"

"Coppy, short for Copperfield because he's one of my favorite magicians. We're still working on a name for Ari. What do you think of Architect? Or Arachna-saurus?"

Brady laughed. "Umm, keep working on it." He blew his nose right into the phone.

Ari changed the subject. "Tell us about your idea

for the club."

"Oh yeah! You're gonna love it, it's so cool! It's gonna be a challenge club," he stated. "You know, we'll take on different challenges."

I could feel my whole body perking up. "I love that!" I said. "Where will we get them from? A textbook or online?" I love math challenges and assumed that's what he meant. I was kind of surprised that this was something Brady would be into because math is definitely not his top subject. But I wasn't about to complain.

We were sitting on the floor in my room leaning against the bed when LuLu came bounding in. She jumped right into my lap and made herself comfortable. She doesn't like to be left out of anything.

"Uh, I don't know. We'll make them up, I guess," Brainy answered. "I don't think they have a textbook with stuff like that in it." He sounded confused.

"What are you talking about? Of course they do," I said, perhaps a bit louder than I should have. "But I don't get how it will work. I mean we're all at different levels."

"Levels? What do you mean? That we're all different heights?" he asked. Ari looked at me, perplexed.

"Heights?" I asked. "Why would that matter?" Now my face matched Ari's.

"Well, suppose you had to jump over a bunch of garbage cans. Of course height would make a difference," he argued.

"Why would we jump over garbage cans?" This conversation was starting to make me feel dizzy. Ari's face looked as confused as I felt.

"I don't know," Brady said. "It doesn't have to be garbage cans. It could be anything. We could jump over puddles or long-jump to see who can go the far-thest."

"So we can guess where we'd land and maybe measure the distance?" Ari asked.

"We probably wouldn't have to measure it," he said. "We'll be able to use our eyeballs and see who went the farthest."

This wasn't making any sense to either of us. "Didn't you say you want to do challenges?" I asked.

"Yeah," he said.

"So why would there be puddles?" Ari asked. "Wouldn't we meet during lunch in the cafeteria? Or at one of our houses after school?"

"Maybe," he said, sounding weary. "Or anywhere we want."

"Well, if we're going to be using textbooks, we'll probably want to do it at school and use theirs. Maybe we can get our hands on a seventh-grade book," I suggested.

"Huh?" Brainy sounded about as lost as we felt.

"Fine, maybe we'll start with the sixth-grade books, but honestly, I don't think they'll be much of a challenge for us. Seventh grade is the place to go for a real challenge."

"Are the seventh-grade books heavier?" he asked.

There was silence for a few moments. I didn't understand why he was having so much difficulty with this concept.

He continued. "Besides, I already told you, there aren't any textbooks for this stuff. We'll make it up as we go."

"What do you mean there are no textbooks? Of course there are!" I practically screamed into the phone. "We use them every day in class!"

"What class? What are you talking about?"

"Um, hello? Math class. Duh! Where else would we be doing challenging math problems?"

There was another long pause as, I suppose, Brainy digested this information. Once it all added up in his head, he laughed hysterically.

"Bahahahaha! We're not gonna do math problems! We're talking about challenges! As in, we take on different dares, like who can jump over a bunch of garbage cans or who can climb the highest. Maybe we'll see who can make it all the way through a scary movie without covering their eyes, or who can make someone freak out and scream when they open their locker. You know, stuff like that. If you're really stuck on the idea of seventh-grade math textbooks, I suppose we could see who can balance the most books on one hand."

"Oh, now I get it!" Ari said. "Maybe we could even do some funny challenges like seeing who can eat their lunch without using their hands!"

I liked that idea but wasn't so thrilled with the idea of watching scary movies.

"But, can some of the challenges be math problems?" I asked, hoping not to be laughed at again. No such luck.

Brainy snorted into the phone. He thought I was kidding but I was one hundred percent serious. "Math problems!" he roared.

"Anyway," he continued, ignoring my suggestion, "that's why I think we should call ourselves the Bravey Cats."

"Yeah, I heard about that but I don't get it," Ari said.

"Same here. What's a Bravey Cat?" I asked.

"You know how someone who's afraid to do things

is called a scaredy cat? We'll be the opposite. We'll be the Bravey Cats since we're going to do stuff that proves we're brave and mighty."

Yeah, I was familiar with the term "scaredy cat." I've been called that, and worse, by my brother and sister. I'm definitely more in the Scaredy Cat camp than the Bravey Cat one. Every summer when we go to the State Fair, my siblings go off together to ride the roller coasters while I hang out at the midway playing games and tracking down the best ice cream.

"Oh. Bravey Cat. That's funny. I like it," I said. At least I could get on board with that part of his idea. I'm not a big risk-taker so I felt a little nervous about joining a group that was all about being brave and mighty. I would have been much more comfortable in a group called the Mighty Mathematicians.

"Great!" he said. "Let's get the group together at lunch tomorrow and talk about the details then."

"Okay," I said, squeezing my eyes shut, hoping that this club wasn't going to be a nightmare for me.

"Sounds good," Ari said. "See you at school."

"Okay, see you,"

"Bye," I said, and hung up.

A challenge club? Bravey Cats? I liked the idea of a club. I loved the job of Chief Nicknamer. But the thought of dares and challenges absolutely terrified me.

"So, what do you want to do now?" I asked Ari, trying not to think about it.

"Let's go down to the basement. In the spirit of our new club, I challenge you to a race. First one there gets to pick what we're doing."

"You're on!" We stood up and LuLu began jumping around our feet.

"On your mark, get set, go!" we shouted together, and ran at top speed out of the room with LuLu yipping, barking, and running along with us.

At least this was a challenge I could handle. I beat him with seconds to spare.

4

Monday Lunch Meeting

The next day, we met up at lunchtime for our club's first official meeting. My buddies and I all sat together at one of the long lunchroom tables.

Brady announced that the first item of business was for me to give everyone their official club nicknames. I came prepared with name tag stickers for everyone to wear so we could remember what to call each other. I stood up and handed each friend their sticker as I revealed their new names. I started with the kids sitting on the side across from me.

"Brady, you are now to be known as Brainy." Brady pointed to his skull and crossed his eyes, making himself look anything but brainy.

"Armando, you are now String Cheese." Armando stopped peeling the plastic wrapper from the string cheese he was holding, and held it up to show us all. There were three more on the table in front of him.

He shrugged and said, "Yeah, that holds up, I guess."

I continued down the line. "Ari, you are going to be Archie."

"Yeah, yeah," he said, not bothering to look up as he continued eating his hard-boiled egg.

"Morgan, would you prefer your new name to be Buzzy or Spike?" I came prepared with two name tags. Morgan has super short hair, which often stands straight up like spikes, but every now and then it's so short that it's more like a buzz cut. Everyone knew what I was referring to.

"Buzzy," Morgan answered, nodding approvingly.

Micah reached across the table and ran his hand across the top of Morgan's soft, fuzzy head. "Buzzy! That's perfect!" he said.

Morgan chuckled.

Then I got to my side of the table.

"Patrick, we're going to call you Tricky." He smiled with his whole freckly face. Patrick is tall, skinny, and has reddish-orangey hair. He often reminds me of a giraffe. I had considered giving him the name Giraffe, but thought he might consider it an insult, so I went with Tricky.

I pointed to Demetrius. "Demetrius, we're shortening your name to Meat." He gave me a salute like we were in the army, and a huge smile. His bright white teeth practically sparkled against his dark brown skin. Next, I turned to my good friend Micah Salzman and introduced him as Salty.

"From your last name," I explained. Then I pointed to myself and said, "And I'm Coppy." I was surprised that no one asked me why I chose that name for myself. Maybe they thought I wanted to be a police officer or something.

I finished by stating the rules, which I had made up, in a very formal, official voice.

"You must use your nicknames when we have our club meetings. You may *not* use them with anyone who is not in the club, and you should *never* use the nicknames outside of club time unless you are speaking with another member about club business. Thumbs-up if you understand and agree."

Everyone in the group gave the thumbs-up sign.

Next, Brainy stood up to present his idea of making this a challenge club. So far, he had told only me and Archie about his plan. "And we're going to call ourselves the Bravey Cats," he announced. He sat back in his seat, looking proud of himself for coming up with that name, and looked around for everyone's approval.

My friends looked confused.

"What's a Bravey Cat?" String Cheese asked.

"No idea," said Salty.

Everyone but Archie and me appeared to be totally baffled.

Just as Brainy was about to explain, Ellie and a few of her friends approached our table. They plopped their lunches down and swung their legs over the benches to sit with us. The eight of us looked at each other, wondering who was going to say something to them first. As the girls began unzipping their lunchboxes or digging into the school hot lunches on their trays, Brainy said, "Sorry, this is a closed meeting."

The girls all laughed.

"Very funny," Megan said, without looking up from her bowl of soup.

"No, I'm being serious," Brainy said. The rest of us pretended to be fascinated by the tasty morsels in front of us.

Ellie and her friends all looked at him as if he was wearing nothing but his underwear.

"Excuse me?" Ellie said with a disbelieving chuckle while emptying the contents of her lunchbox onto the table. I watched her unload a sandwich, a banana, and a container of Mom's applesauce. (We apparently had moved into Project Applesauce Phase Two overnight!) I wondered if it was the same banana I had seen on her bedroom floor the night before.

"Yeah, sorry, you can't sit here today," Meat agreed. "We're having a meeting."

"Yeah, right," Megan said, laughing. She put her hands up to make air quotes. "You're having 'a meeting!'"

None of the Bravey Cats said a word.

One by one, the girls' smiles and giggles turned into frowns and angry glares. Ellie looked directly at me with furrowed eyebrows while lifting her sandwich to her mouth. She didn't have to say a word. I knew exactly what she was thinking: *What's going on here, YoYo?*

"You're kidding, right?" Either Marissa or Sophie Klein asked with a sharp, angry edge. (Sometimes I refer to them as either Marophie or Sophissa because they are identical twins and I can never tell which one is which. I'm so glad that even though Ellie and I are twins, people have no trouble telling us apart.) This was twin Marophie.

"No, for real!" Tricky said proudly, chomping on some chips that left an orange residue on his lips, and which kind of matched the color of his hair. He didn't seem to catch on that the girls were upset. "We're having the first-ever meeting of our new club, and the meeting is only open to club members." He popped another chip, then added, "But you can sit here tomorrow. We won't be meeting then."

"Wait!" Ellie said, her ears once again giving her away. Whenever she's embarrassed or angry, they turn color, first a dark shade of pink, then as red as if they were sunburned. "We can't sit here because we're not in your club?" Whoa. They took on a color I'd never seen before.

"Why not?" Sophissa, the other twin, asked looking around the table, glaring angrily at each of the Cats. "Is it because we're girls?"

Marophie added to her sister's accusation. "Are you saying this is a boys-only club?"

"Um, hello!" Buzzy waved at the girls. "I'm in the group, and I'm not a boy."

Ever since the start of this school year, Morgan has asked us to please use the pronoun "they" instead of "she." I had never met anyone who didn't go by he or she before, but Morgan explained to us that they'd prefer to be called "they" because they didn't really feel like a boy or a girl. I don't exactly understand how that feels, but I've always liked Morgan and it didn't really make a difference to me or to any of our other friends. Morgan is just Morgan. Well, now Morgan is Buzzy too!

"Yeah, Morgan's in the club," Brainy practically shouted.

The tone of this encounter was escalating to a very uncomfortable level. It was true, pretty much all of Ellie's friends were girls and my friends were boys, except for Morgan.

I looked at the girls' expressions at the other end of the table and started to feel like I was being squeezed in on all sides. I felt my own face getting red hot the same way that Ellie's ears do. My face can turn such a deep shade of red that all the freckles that are normally there kind of disappear. I knew I had to calm things down before they got out of hand and I ended up looking like a brown-haired tomato.

"Of course it's not a boys-only club!" I blurted out. "Why wouldn't we let girls into the group? That's completely ridiculous. Haven't you ever been in a club before? We just wanted to have our own private club with our friends. That's all."

"So let us join," Sophissa said, fuming.

Meat spoke up next. "But this is our group of friends. You've never wanted to hang out with us before."

"Like, ever," Salty agreed.

"Yeah, and you don't even know what our club is about," Archie added.

"I can tell you what it isn't," I said, jumping in. "It's *not* the Corey McNuggets Fan Club, that's for sure."

Archie agreed, "Definitely not!"

Although Ellie and I hang out together at home, when we're with our friends, we rarely have anything to do with each other. We just don't have a lot of interests in common. She and her friends love to talk about Corey McDonald, day in and day out. My friends and I have no patience or desire to talk about him or to listen to his "music."

"There's more to us than merely being Corey fans. You know that," Ellie said indignantly. "And stop making fun of him. He's awesome and you know it."

I laughed out loud. Some of the other guys at the table snickered too.

"Anyway, why would you want to join a club that you know nothing about?" Archie asked. "Maybe you'd hate it." I chuckled quietly to myself, realizing that most of the real club members didn't know what it was all about yet either.

"Or maybe we'd love it," Ellie said, her ears flaming red. "So tell us, what is it?"

Archie got quiet and pointed to Brainy, indicating that he was the one in charge.

"It's a challenge club," Brainy said, looking very

pleased with himself. "And we're calling ourselves the Bravey Cats because we're brave and mighty, and we're going to take on all sorts of challenges."

"What's a Bravey Cat?" Camille asked.

"It's the opposite of a Scaredy Cat," Brainy answered, rolling his eyes as if he'd explained it a million times already.

These details were as new to the other club members as they were to Ellie and her friends, but everyone nodded as if this was old news.

"Sounds kind of dopey," Stephanie said.

"Yeah, you know what? You were right. I'm not interested," said Camille. "See ya."

"I'm out," Sophie and Marissa said at the same time, and then giggled about speaking in sync.

And without much of a commotion, the girls got up and moved to the next table over. That is, all the girls except for Ellie, Megan, and a girl I didn't know very well named Asha. She started at our school in September. I'd noticed her because she's one of a handful of girls who wear a scarf-like head covering called a hijab. She pretty much only hangs out with the girls, and I'd never spoken to her before.

"A challenge club? I love it!" Ellie exclaimed, taking a bite out of her Swiss cheese, cucumber, and hummus sandwich (her new favorite), clearly having no intention of leaving. "I'm all about challenges. Count me in."

"I'd try it," Asha said with a shrug. I was surprised by this. Asha seemed quiet and shy, so I assumed she'd leave with the other girls. Maybe she stayed because she wanted to make new friends.

"Me too," Megan, Ellie's best friend, declared. "I'm in." She dipped her grilled cheese sandwich into the cup of hot tomato soup on her tray.

"Well, who said you could join just like that?" Meat demanded. "It's not like you're a part of our friend group."

"Yeah," String Cheese said. "You can't just decide you're in and then you're in. It doesn't work that way."

Ellie continued chewing. "Why not?"

Brainy glanced at each of us with a look that I took to mean, *"Leave it to me, I'll get rid of them."*

"Fine," he said. "If you want to join, you're gonna have to do something to prove that you're worthy of being a Bravey Cat. We're going to be challenging each other to different dares. If you want to be one of us, you have to do what we challenge you to do, no matter what it is." He looked around at the group with a smug air, as if to say, *"That oughta do it!"*

There was an awkward silence as the three girls stared at Brainy.

"Cool," my sister said, taking another bite of her sandwich. "Bring it on. What do we have to do?"

This caught Brainy off guard. "Uh," he said, looking around the room, stalling, and trying to come up with some sort of dare that would scare the girls off. "Uh," he said again.

The eight of us looked at one another in a sort of panic. We never expected this scenario. Since when did the girls want to hang out with us? We had to figure out a way to get rid of them. But how?

5

I Won't and You Can't Make Me

Hold on. We need a group conference. Bravey Cats, huddle up," Brainy announced.

Like a football team on the ten-yard line, the eight of us all leaned our heads in toward the middle of the table, away from Ellie, Asha, and Megan.

"We can't let them in! What can we do to make them not want to be in the club?" Brainy whispered while wiping his nose with a tissue. "Any ideas?"

"Maybe...let's make them skip around the lunchroom," Tricky suggested. "They'll be too embarrassed to do that."

"Or make it even more humiliating. Make them skip around the lunchroom while flapping their arms and making loud monkey noises," String Cheese said.

"Nah, we want to get rid of them but we don't want to get them in trouble," Archie said. "Ms. Amato would throw a fit." We're supposed to stay in our seats when we're in the lunchroom except to go to the bathroom, get more food, or throw our trash away. Ms. Amato is the teacher who is always on lunch duty, and who, we joke, has eyes in the back of her head. We can't get away with anything when she's around. We call her Ms. Tomato behind her back, even though it's not very nice.

"How about if we make them eat something gross?" Buzzy offered.

"Yeah, I like that! Something like chocolate covered crickets or fried spiders!" Meat exclaimed.

"Brilliant idea," Buzzy said sarcastically. "I just happen to have fried spiders in my lunch today." Buzzy took a moment for a huge eye-roll. "I meant, like, something we could make them eat right now."

"Yeah, that's good," Brainy said, with an approving smirk. "Okay, leave it to me, I know what to do."

And without anyone giving any directions, we all clapped our hands and yelled, "Break!" just like a real football team. We sat back down in our seats.

Brainy said to the girls, "As Bravey Cats, we're going to take on dares and challenges. If you want to join us, we dare you to take a bite of everyone's lunch at this table and eat it all together at once."

The girls wrinkled their noses in disgust.

"No way," Megan said, shaking her head.

"Why not?" Brainy teased. "Are you chicken?" He tucked his hands into his armpits, flapped his elbows, and made chicken noises. "Bak, bak, bak!"

"No," Megan said calmly.

"Vegetarian?" Tricky asked with genuine curiosity.

"No," she replied.

"Well," Meat asked, "are you a Bravey Cat or a Scaredy Cat?"

"It's honestly about the germs," Megan replied, her voice sounding more annoyed than grossed out. "I can't bite all of your food. That would be unhealthy."

"She's right," Tricky agreed, nodding to Brainy.

"Fine. Everyone will break off a piece of whatever they're eating. Then you have to eat it all mushed up together."

"Okay," Megan said, "I can do that."

"Nope," said Ellie, looking around at all the different foods on the table. "I can't."

"Why?" Brainy taunted. "Are *you* chicken?"

I knew where this was heading. I was going to jump in but I knew that Ellie could stand up for herself. Besides, she answered so quickly I couldn't possibly have responded fast enough even if I tried.

"Oh, I'm not afraid," Ellie said with confidence, "I just can't do it. And you can't make someone do something like that. What if I had a peanut allergy? Demetrius is eating peanut butter!"

"Well, do you have a peanut allergy?" Brainy asked, eyeing Meat's PB and J sandwich.

"I do not," she replied.

"So?" Brainy crossed his arms.

"So, you can't make people eat things that they can't eat. I keep kosher." She paused and looked at me, "*We* keep kosher."

"What does that mean exactly?" String Cheese asked.

"Well, we're Jewish," she began, "and there are rules for Jewish people about what we can and can't eat. It's called keeping kosher."

"I'm Jewish too, but my family doesn't keep kosher," Salty said.

"Yeah, some families keep kosher and some don't," Ellie explained patiently. "Our family does." She pointed at the sandwich Tricky was holding. "Patrick is eating what looks like ham and cheese, and I can't eat ham. I also don't mix meat with dairy products, so I couldn't eat Armando's string cheese along with whatever that is," she said, pointing at the meat-filled sandwich Brainy had in his thick hands.

"I can't eat ham either," Asha practically whispered. "I only eat foods that are halal, and ham is not halal."

"What's halal?" Tricky looked like he was going to fall over with all this new information coming at him.

Asha looked down at the table, seeming a bit overwhelmed and a little embarrassed. I felt kind of bad that she was so shy. I guess Archie did too because he spoke up to help her out. "It's kind of like how keeping kosher is for Jewish people but those are the food rules for people who are Muslim. Right, Asha?"

She nodded, flashing a big grin at him, seeming pleased to be understood.

"That's too bad," Brainy said smugly. "I guess you can't be in the club then."

I jumped out of my seat. "No way, Brainy! That is not okay!"

He looked at me confused as if to say, *I thought you didn't want them in the group either.*

I continued. "I have no problem giving them a dare to get into the group but you can't make someone do something that goes against their religion!"

We had just discussed this at Shul School with Rabbi Green the previous morning. We were talking about Hanukkah and how Judah Maccabee and his tiny group of fighters stood up against the big, strong Greek army. The terrible king Antiochus and his followers tried to make the Jews give up their traditions, like keeping kosher and studying *Torah*—the stories, laws, and teachings of the Jewish people. They forced the Jews to pray to the Greek gods and even to sacrifice and eat pigs. I felt my inner-Judah Maccabee radiating from inside of me.

"So what do you suggest, Coppy?" Brainy asked, growing impatient.

"I'm good with the mushed up food dare, but it can't include stuff they can't eat." I looked around to see what everyone else had in front of them. "I think that if we skip Tricky's ham and cheese, and your roast beef—or whatever that is—all three of them can do it. Why don't the two of you put in some of your dessert instead?"

Brainy looked sad. "But I have chocolate pudding! I don't want to give up my pudding!" he whined.

"Well, this was your idea!" I said. "If you don't want to put in your chocolate pudding, how about some of your celery sticks?

"Fine by me!" he answered, tossing three sticks down on the table, one at a time.

Then I spoke directly to the girls.

"That should do it, right? Anything else here that you can't eat?" Of course, I knew what Ellie could and couldn't eat, but I didn't know about Megan, and certainly didn't know all the rules that Asha followed.

The three of them scanned the table and, one by one, they each announced their approval. Buzzy went up to the front of the lunchroom and brought back three bowls for them.

"To keep it fair, even though Megan can eat Tricky's and Brainy's food, let's make it so that all three girls get the exact same items," I suggested.

We passed the three bowls around and all "donated" something from our lunches into them. Then Brainy, Meat, and Salty each took a bowl, covered all the food with napkins, and punched and smashed the stuff inside. When they lifted the napkins, it looked like somebody had already chewed it up and spit it all back out. It was so gross I could barely look at it without wanting to barf.

Next, they mixed up the smushed food with a spoon and presented each of the girls with a bowl filled with brownish-greenish slop. It was a mish-mash of tomato soup; cucumber, hummus, and Swiss cheese sandwich; peanut butter and jelly sandwich; macaroni and cheese; yogurt, celery sticks, banana, potato chips—and Mom's applesauce. We watched in horror as they dug their spoons into the nasty glop and each took a gag-worthy bite.

"Done!" Megan declared victoriously, throwing her arms in the air.

"What do you mean, 'done'? You're not done!" Meat said.

"Right," Salty declared, "you have to eat the whole thing!"

"And no spitting it out, either!" Archie added. "You need to swallow it all down!"

The Bravey Cats gave a unanimous thumbs-up. Megan, Asha, and Ellie made grossed-out faces at one another, shrugged in surrender, and then slowly lifted their spoons from the table. Ellie actually closed her eyes, took a deep breath, leaned over the bowl, and dove in, snarfing down the mush in a matter of seconds. Megan and Asha, on the other hand, slowly but steadily chipped away at theirs, making faces with each bite they took. I really did gag a couple of times watching them. When they completed the dare, they each threw their spoons down into the empty bowls and grinned at us.

The original club members looked at one another in shock and maybe even a little awe.

"Man, that was nasty," String Cheese said.

"I can't believe you really did it," Meat said. "I almost puked just watching you!"

Brainy announced, "Bravey Cats, group meeting!" Once again we huddled up over the table, leaning away from the girls.

"What do we do now?" Brainy asked nervously.

"What do you mean, 'what do we do now?'" Buzzy replied. "We let them in! They took on that disgusting dare and they all did it. They're Bravey Cats now, like it or not."

"I agree," Tricky said.

"Me too," I said. "I don't love the idea of sharing the club with my sister, but a deal's a deal."

"They beat us at our own game," Archie said. "What's fair is fair."

"I never thought they'd actually do it," Brainy groaned.

"Same here," I said. "It never occurred to me that they'd seriously want to join, but I guess we don't have a choice now."

We all looked at each other, shrugged, and then Brainy called out, "One, two, three..."

"Break!" we all yelled, and we sat back down.

I was honestly shocked that the girls had any interest in joining our club, although the truth of the matter is that, between the two of us, Ellie is the one who's more likely to take on risks and challenges. As much as I didn't want to admit it, it made more sense for her to be in the club than for me.

"I guess that makes it official," Brainy said with a sigh. "You're all Bravey Cats now."

"Cool!" Megan said.

"Thanks," Ellie added.

Asha smiled proudly.

"Looks like I'll need to come up with nicknames for the three of you. I'll think about it and get back to you," I said. Then I reintroduced everyone by their new names to our new members, and explained the rules about using them.

"Can we please get started now?" Archie asked. "Lunch is almost over!"

Brainy stood up, sniffled, puffed out his chest and sucked in his stomach. All this made him appear very much in charge. He knocked on the table three times to officially start the meeting, "The Bravey Cats Club is officially in session!" he declared, sounding more like the coach of a high school football team than a fifth-grader in the lunchroom. "The first thing we need to do is set up some rules. And we need to vote on everything. You have to vote either in favor of something or against it. Okay? All in favor of voting for everything, say 'Eyeball.'"

"Eyeball?" Tricky said with a chuckle, "I thought it's supposed to be 'All in favor, say Aye'!"

"Yeah, but I want to say 'Eyeball' instead. It's our club, we can do whatever we want." Brainy repeated, "All in favor, say 'Eyeball.'"

"Eyeball!" we all declared, mixed in with a few giggles.

Brainy continued by slapping his hand on the table. "We'll meet every Monday and Friday at lunchtime at this table. Of course, we'll probably end up eating together on other days too, but Mondays and Fridays will be our official meeting time." Then he ended with, "And no outsiders are allowed when we're meeting. All in favor, say 'Eyeball.'"

"Eyeball!" we all declared again, with even more gusto.

"And you must use your given nicknames at the meetings," I added.

Everyone shouted, "Eyeball!"

And with that, the first ever meeting of the Bravey Cats club was officially, finally, in session.

6

What Did I Get Myself Into?

The bell rang, which meant that lunch was over, but we had only just gotten started with our club time and wanted to continue. It was time for recess, so we agreed to move the meeting outside to the playground. This year we have recess with just the kids in the fifth and sixth grades. Most of the time we play kickball or tag or some other running-around game on the field. We don't spend as much time on the monkey bars, swings, and slides as we used to when we were younger, so we pretty much had the whole place to ourselves, other than some of the sixth-grade girls sitting around and hanging out on top of the climbing set.

Brainy, Megan, Buzzy, and Ellie sat on the swings while the rest of us sat on the ground.

Brainy pulled a tissue from the never-ending supply in his pocket. He had a whole stash in there that were connected one to the other and it reminded me of the magician gag where you start with a colorful scarf and it's tied to the next one and the next one until you end up with a whole, long string of connected scarves. He shook out the crumpled tissue, blew his nose with a loud honk and announced, "Now that we've got all the membership stuff out of the way, let's figure out the ground rules and share ideas for the group."

Buzzy said, "I'm excited about doing challenges and dares. I think they're going to be fun. They can be silly

or goofy, but we shouldn't do anything that's dangerous or mean."

"Yeah, if we're not comfortable doing something,
we shouldn't have to," I agreed immediately. I loved
that Buzzy brought this up and I didn't have to.

"Okay," Archie jumped in, "but, it *is* a challenge
club. The idea is to push yourself to do something you
might not normally do. Or to try to break your own
record. So, no one should have to do anything they
think isn't a good idea or isn't safe, but I think we
should all push ourselves a little."

"Yeah, that's fair," Buzzy agreed.

"That's why we're going to vote on everything,"
Brainy explained.

"That makes sense," Ellie said.

I figured it was a good time to try my idea out on
the group. Just because Brainy didn't like it, didn't
mean that the others wouldn't.

"You know what I think would be super cool? If we
try to do some really, really hard and *challenging* math
problems." Unfortunately, everyone except for Ari and
Ellie absolutely cracked up. My best friend and my
twin sister know me better than anyone else on this
planet, so they knew that I truly meant it. The rest of
the group thought I was joking.

"Good one, Coppy!" Meat said with a big smile.

"Hysterical! That's why we also call you Jokin' Joel,"
Tricky agreed, shaking his head with a chuckle.

I love it when people think I'm funny, but it was
frustrating that hardly anyone realized that I was actually being serious. I wanted to say something but figured I'd only get laughed at again. There's nothing better than getting a good laugh from a joke or a prank,
but it's never any fun when *you* are the butt of the joke

and everyone's laughing *at* you. So I kept my mouth shut.

"Let's get started with the dares and challenges already," Salty said. "So, Brady—" I held up my hand to stop him and pointed at the name tag, which Brady had now stuck to the outside of his puffy blue jacket. Salty corrected himself. "Right, I mean, Brainy, how about if you start us off?"

"This'll be a short one. I challenge you all to a breath-holding contest. Let's see who can hold their breath the longest."

"Yes! Let's start with that," I agreed with enthusiasm. This was much more my speed. Not too scary at all!

"Okay, on the count of three, hold your breath," Brainy said. "One, two, three, go!" We each got up, took in a giant gulp of air, and stood around in a circle looking goofy, with our cheeks blown up and sticking out like human pufferfish. YaYa's face turned pink and then red, the same way her ears do, and mine probably did too. One by one, each member of the group dropped out with a huge exhale and sat down on the ground where they were standing. Asha and I were the last ones left. With our cheeks still puffed out, we stood facing one another. I crossed my arms in front of my chest to make myself look tough. She put her hands on her hips to do the same. My eyes started tearing up. Asha's nose began to flare a little.

It was a long, hard-fought battle. I held on for as long as I could, but after a couple more seconds I couldn't take it anymore. Feeling a little lightheaded, I let out the air in my cheeks and took a deep breath. Then, like a referee in a boxing match, Buzzy took Asha's hand, raised it over her head, and announced,

"The winner!" Asha looked surprised but pleased.

I was disappointed but said, "Nice job!" while huffing and puffing.

Being a good sport, she said, "Thanks, good effort!" She was huffing a little herself. I nodded, still trying to breathe normally. We both sat down in the circle with the rest of the kids.

Brainy stood up and said, "Okay, before we go on to any more challenges, let's discuss the homework assignment for this week."

"Homework?" String Cheese said, looking alarmed. "I didn't sign up for homework!"

"Yeah, I'm in charge and I'm giving out homework," Brainy answered. "Everyone has to come to the next meeting with at least two ideas of challenges for the group. One should be simple, like the holding-our-breath challenge we just did, and the other should be a super-duper challenging dare. Holding our breath is fine, but as Bravey Cats we need to do things that show how brave we are."

"I don't get it. What kind of challenges do they need to be?" Megan asked.

"Anything at all that feels like something that you might not normally do, or that might be scary or hard. Like for example..." Brainy stopped and thought for a moment. "I dare you to kiss Ms. Tomato's shoes. Something like that. Dares can be for the whole group or for one person at a time."

"How about something like riding Dead Man's Drop water slide at Splash World?" Ellie asked. "Because I've already done that, and I can tell you that it's almost poop-in-your-pants scary. You want to test your bravery? Put that on your list!"

"Yeah," Brainy said, "that's a good one."

"Dibs!" Ellie called out, raising her hand like she was in class. "I get to put 'ride a scary water slide' as my first dare! I like this kind of homework."

"Yeah, this is definitely homework I can deal with," String Cheese chimed in.

Megan turned to Brainy. "Hey, Brady," then she quickly corrected herself, noticing his name tag, "I mean, Brainy. If you're giving out homework, can you make it an official homework assignment for—" she stopped and squinted at my name tag, which I had also moved to my jacket "—Coppy to come up with nicknames for me, Ellie, and Asha?"

"Good idea," I acknowledged before Brainy had time to respond. "I'm on it."

Meanwhile, everyone else started to brainstorm ideas for dares and challenges. Some were athletic challenges like running a mile without stopping, or shooting hoops and getting twenty baskets in a row. Those sounded hard but fun. Other dares included crazy ideas like going to math class with underwear on our heads, or wearing all our clothes inside out. But when I heard Salty suggest watching a scary horror movie in a dark room alone, I started to panic.

What other "super-duper" challenges would the other kids come up with? There was no way on earth you'd ever catch me even climbing up the steps to Dead Man's Drop, let alone actually going down it. When Ellie did it, I thought I was going to hurl just watching from the sidelines.

Everyone jabbered on excitedly about their ideas. I, on the other hand, despite the cold December temperatures, broke into a sweat.

What did I get myself into?

7

Might As Well Jump

Since Brainy had given out a homework assignment, a bunch of us thought we were done with the day's meeting, so we got up and started to walk toward the field to join the kickball game. But Brainy had different plans for us.

He held his gloved hands up to his mouth and called, "Hey, Bravey Cats! Come back! Let's do more challenges today. We can play kickball anytime, but Mondays and Fridays are reserved for Bravey Cat activities. Let's plan on meeting at recess each week too."

Everyone said, "Eyeball!" without being asked.

Brainy continued. "Pick a challenge for us all to do on the playground. Everyone has to come up with their own original idea."

Archie challenged us to see who could swing the highest in 30 seconds. There are only four swings so we had to take turns and do a few rounds. The winner, after all the rounds, was Buzzy.

Ellie challenged everyone to hang upside down from the monkey bars, and the one who could last the longest would win. Asha won that contest, which was a double challenge because while she was hanging upside down, she was holding her hijab so it wouldn't cover up her face. She definitely deserved that win.

I challenged everyone to see who could travel fastest across the monkey bars hanging by their hands.

Meat, who is a gymnast, left us in the dust. He was crazy fast!

Brainy challenged us to jump off the top of the climbing structure. It didn't seem like the smartest idea ever, especially since it was still a little wet from yesterday's and this morning's pitiful snowfall, but I was willing to give it a try, so I went first. I took the little ladder on the side up to the narrow, wobbly bridge. I ran across the bridge. Next, I got down on my hands and knees and crawled through the tunnel, which left me off right where the sixth-grade girls were sitting. They kind of snarled at me, annoyed that I was in their space. I ignored them, turned back around to hop on top of the tunnel that I had just emerged from. I carefully turned around and climbed on top of the roof above the sixth-grade girls' heads. I crawled over the top to the very edge, stood up and shouted.

"Look out below!"

I jumped down and landed in the wood chips. I'm pretty sure I landed on my feet but found myself on my back, watching the white, fluffy clouds float by in the blue sky above me.

"Nice job, Joel!" I heard my friends call out to me.

From the ground I called back and corrected them, "Coppy!"

After I caught my breath, I sat up, brushed the wood chips off of my jacket and pants, and called out, "Who's next?"

One by one, my club-mates took their turns carefully climbing up the structure and making their way to the very top. They each stood on the edge and readied themselves to leap.

When Archie jumped, he flapped his arms like they were wings and shouted, "Look at me! I'm flying!" Most impressively, he landed right on his feet with his knees bent. He stood up straight, threw his arms up in the air and sang out, "Tada!" like a gymnast who had stuck the landing.

That got Meat, the actual gymnast, excited to do his own jump. I wondered if he'd attempt one of his gymnastics flips. The thought of it made me a little nervous but excited at the same time. I watched him shimmy his way across the top and set himself up to jump.

I'm not sure what happened next. Maybe his foot slipped or he simply jumped badly, but a few moments later, Meat was curled up in a ball on the ground, screaming and crying in pain. He held on to his ankle and shouted for one of us to get a teacher.

"Oh no!" Ellie cried out. "I hope it's not broken!" She had recently recovered from a broken arm, although she hadn't done anything nearly as exciting as jumping off the top of a playset. She tripped over a stick or a rock or something one night when she was out with Mom walking LuLu. But I have no doubt that she knew the pain Meat was in.

Megan ran to get a teacher. Within minutes, she returned with Ms. Russo.

"Demetrius, can you sit up?" Ms. Russo asked gently.

"I think so," he said in a weak voice, tears streaming down his face. I'd never seen Meat cry before. He winced in pain as he lifted his head off the ground and sat straight up, still holding his ankle.

"Can you tell me what happened?" Ms. Russo inquired.

"I slipped off the jungle gym," he said, leaving out the part about climbing onto the very top for the purpose of jumping off.

"Oh my, let's get you inside. We'll have the nurse take a look and see if we need to contact your parents."

Ms. Russo helped him stand up on his good leg. She stood on one side of Meat, and Archie stood on the other. Meat put his arms around both their shoulders while Ms. Russo also held on to his waist. Together they tried to help him hobble off the playground. When they reached the edge of the woodchips, Archie crouched down in front of Meat, who hopped onto Archie's back. Archie carried him away by piggyback. We all looked at one another, not sure of what to do.

"Okay, who wants to go next?" Brainy asked with a sniffle.

"What do you mean?" Buzzy asked in disbelief. "We're not doing this dare anymore! Meat just got hurt. What's wrong with you?"

"Nothing's wrong with me," Brainy replied angrily. "That proves it's a good dare. There are consequences if you don't get it right. Look, if you go to the circus and you see someone walk across a tightrope that's a few inches off the ground, it's not nearly as exciting or impressive as seeing someone do it from way high up in the air. Then if they do it without a net, now that's a *real* challenge!"

I couldn't believe what I was hearing.

"So what are you saying?" Megan asked.

"I'm saying we should keep going. Let's finish the dare," he replied.

My faith in Brainy as a leader was running thin. I wasn't sure he was so great at making good decisions. Luckily, Ms. Russo blew her whistle to let us know it was time to go back inside. I don't think I'd ever been so grateful for recess to be over.

8

How About Some Applesauce?

Ari spends a lot of time at our house. Sometimes he comes over just because, and sometimes he comes over after school when his parents are working and Carolyn isn't available. Carolyn is, as Ari's mom calls her, his "babysitter." I probably don't even need to tell you that he hates that word. Obviously. I mean, come on, we're in fifth grade and clearly he's not a baby. Where did the word "babysitter" come from, anyway? It's not like they actually sit on babies!

Ari's parents are both doctors. They work at different hospitals, and sometimes he needs a place to stay when they're both working late. For example, every year Ari and I look forward to Christmas Eve, which may sound strange since we don't celebrate Christmas. But we get a sleepover because his parents both work that night so the doctors who do celebrate can be home with their families. Then, after their long shift, his parents go home and sleep all day. Last year they were so tired that they let Ari stay over the next night too. Our family custom is to go out for Chinese food on Christmas Eve, so we always plan on getting a table for six instead of for five.

After we had come in from our Bravey Cat recess meeting that day, Ari got a note from the office informing him that Carolyn the "babysitter" was sick and that he was to come home with me on the bus after school. Ari's parents don't ever want him to be home alone, so this happens anytime Carolyn is unavailable. As usual, Dad was working at his bookstore, The Silver Lining, so he wasn't home. My mom, on the other hand, is almost always around in the afternoons. She's an artist and works at home in her studio upstairs in the attic.

The first thing we did when we got home was make a quick snack of frozen waffles with—you guessed it— applesauce on the side. It was my first opportunity of the year to sample Mom's famous applesauce, since I hadn't taken any for lunch. It was exactly as I always remembered it: a little chunky—but not too chunky— with cinnamon mixed in, as well as Mom's secret ingredient: a hint of maple syrup. Delicious!

We hardly had any real homework beyond the assignment we got for the Bravey Cats at recess. We sat at the kitchen table, ate, and did our math and reading assignments, and within thirty minutes we were done. I love light-homework days!

Next, we called Meat to see how he was doing. Unfortunately for him, he had, indeed, sprained his ankle.

"Oh no, Meat, I'm so sorry," I said to him over the phone. (We had decided to count this as official club business, so we went with the nicknames.)

"Yeah, me too," Archie added.

"Thanks, guys," Meat replied. "It especially stinks because I have a gymnastics meet next week." Then he added sadly, "I guess I should say, I *had* a meet next week." We felt bad for him, and a little guilty too.

We talked to Meat for a little while, and when we got off the phone, Ari and I headed to the basement so I could show him my new juggling skills. Before going down, we stopped at the top of the stairs so I could warn him to adjust his expectations.

"Don't be too harsh on me," I said. "I'm really a beginner, so I still practice using bean bags. I'm planning to put together a Hanukkah-themed show for my whole family when they come over for our big Hanukkah party. I'll do some juggling, a little magic, and maybe even some stand-up comedy."

"Maybe you could juggle candles," Ari suggested.

"Yeah, but Hanukkah candles are pretty thin, and it might be hard to catch them without breaking them," I said. "It's much easier to work with something less breakable, like balls or metal rings."

"You know," he said, "I've seen professional jugglers toss around things like plates and tennis rackets. I once saw a juggler toss a bunch of bowling pins, and then her assistant threw in a bowling ball! I've even seen them juggle lit torches! Maybe someday you'll get that good at it."

"Yeah, maybe. But for now, trying to juggle *unlit* candles seems like enough of a challenge. Can you imagine if I could juggle lit Hanukkah candles? Now that would be awesome!"

We made it about halfway down to the basement when I heard the lock on the front door open. I ran back upstairs to the foyer to see Dad walking in.

"Hi, Dad!" I shouted, jumping into his arms for a hug. "You're home so early!"

"Whoa! You're acting like I've been away at sea for months. I've just been at the store."

The Silver Lining is close to our house, which is really convenient, especially this time of year. Even before Thanksgiving comes, Dad practically lives at the store because so many people buy gifts there for Christmas, Hanukkah, and other winter holidays. All through December, he leaves the house before the sun comes up to open the store extra early, and doesn't finish until long after dark. He usually comes home for a quick dinner and goes back to the store. In the two weeks leading up to Christmas, he often brings dinner with him and stays until it's time for him to come home and get ready for bed. Many nights, Mom goes there too and stays to help until closing time.

"Well, we don't get to see you all that much now that it's December," I noted.

"Yeah, I know, bud. Sorry about that. And I'm not sticking around now either. I need to grab something quickly from my desk and get right back." He turned toward Ari. "Hi, Ari!"

"Hi, Mr. Silver."

Dad gave him a stern look. He didn't have to say anything at all. Ari said, "I mean, hi," but then practically swallowed Dad's first name, "Mark." It was so quiet we could barely hear him, but it satisfied Dad.

"That's better!" Dad said with a smile, and he gave Ari a one-armed hug.

"Hi, honey. What are you doing home? Everything okay?" Mom asked, coming down the stairs from her studio.

"Oh yeah, just picking something up," he said.

As soon as Mom realized that nothing was wrong, but before he even finished his sentence, she rushed to the kitchen and then hurried back to the foyer with a little bowl of applesauce.

"Ah, so we're eating the applesauce now, I see," Dad said with a chuckle. "Made too much again this year, Deb?" he asked, with his eyes crinkling at the corners.

Mom gave him a playful punch in the arm. "Yes, a little," she replied with a laugh. It's literally the same exact situation every single year. "How're things at the store?"

"Busy!" Dad said happily. "I should probably bring something with me for dinner. It may very well be a long night."

Dad scraped the bowl with his spoon, scooping out every last drop. "Delicious, as always," he said, handing the bowl back to Mom. Then he popped into his office, which is right off the foyer, took some papers from his desk, and announced, "All right, everybody, I'm heading back to the salt mines." He often makes weird comments like that. Sometimes I need a translator for his Dad-isms. This one, I've learned, means that he needs to get back to work. I think when most people say it, they mean that they have to drag themselves back to work. Lucky for Dad, he actually loves his job, so going back to work is a good thing.

Since people like to buy stuff online these days, Dad is always coming up with fun ways to get people into the store. He has special guests, including authors who come in to read from their books, talk about them, and answer questions. He always has hot coffee, cookies, and other treats for shoppers on a table in the back.

One time on Cinco de Mayo he hired a Mariachi band that played on the sidewalk outside the store. He's had Irish Celtic dancers for St. Patrick's Day, tapping and clogging right in front of the big store window. He even had a mime outside once, who messed around with the passersby. The mime pretended to take a woman's shopping bags and to drink a little kid's milkshake. Of course he didn't really do those things, but his shenanigans caught people's attention, and before long they were tempted to check out what was inside The Silver Lining.

Thinking about the bookstore gave me an idea. I followed Dad into the kitchen.

"Hey, Dad, do you need any help at the store? Maybe Archduke Franz Ferdinand and I will come with you." Yeah, I was still messing around with new names for Ari. Even though I announced to the group that his new name would be Archie, I was having too much fun coming up with even more nicknames for my best bud. I couldn't stop now.

"I'd love that," Dad replied, not reacting the slightest bit to the crazy name I just called my pal. He opened the refrigerator door and peeked in.

"I'll come and help, too!" Ellie said, running into the kitchen. "I'm all done with my homework. We didn't get much today."

"Great!" Dad said, his voice muffled from inside the refrigerator. "I'll take all the help I can get. You okay with me stealing the kids for a little while before dinner, Deb?"

"Sure," she answered. "Mark, why don't you take the leftover mushroom barley soup from last night. That should fill you up a bit. And kids, you can take a healthy snack with you. How about some—"

"Applesauce!" we all said at the same time and then laughed.

"Ari, I'll tell your mom to pick you up over there when she's ready to get you, okay?" Mom said.

"What say you, Archduke? Wanna help my dad at the bookstore for a little while?"

"Okay, sure."

"Okay, sure, what?" I asked, working up to another jab at him. "Okay to us going to the store or to me calling you Archduke Franz Ferdinand?"

Ari sighed. "Okay, to the store. And I give up—I don't care anymore about the nicknames!"

"So I can call you anything I want?" I asked with a mischievous grin, rubbing my hands together like an evil scientist in the movies.

"Sure, whatever. I don't care!"

Heh, heh, heh, I thought. *Challenge accepted!*

9

Soup and Bunny-Oats

The Silver Lining is one of my favorite places on Earth. I love everything about it, starting with the little "ting-ting" sound the bells on the door make when it swings open. When Ellie and I were really young and Jeremy was in kindergarten, he told us it was the sound of a tiny invisible book fairy greeting everyone as they entered. I'm embarrassed to tell you that I believed it for way longer than I should have.

I love how, the moment you step inside the shop, the sweet, crisp, inviting scent of books wafts into your nose. Some people like the smell of a brand new car. Mom says that she likes the way babies' heads smell. (Weird!) For me, it's always been the scent of books, and specifically, the smell of Dad's bookshop. Maybe it's because I've been going there since I was a newborn and it's like my second home, or maybe it's because I love to read so much. Or maybe I love to read so much because a bookstore is my second home.

At this time of year, Dad decorates the whole store for winter and all the seasonal holidays. Sparkly, silvery snowflakes hang from the ceiling. Strings of little white lights are draped over the bookshelves and around the windows. An electric Hanukkah *menorah*, the special candle holder we use for Hanukkah, sits in the front window. Next to it is a miniature Christmas tree. On the other side of the tree is a different candle holder. Dad told me it's called a *kinara*, and it's for the holiday of Kwanzaa. He also sets up a row of *diyas*—little oil lamps made from clay that one of his customers brought him from India for the Hindu holiday of Diwali. Even though our family celebrates Hanukkah, I love that he puts up decorations for all the different holidays.

I stood in the middle of the store, closed my eyes, and took in a deep whiff. Ahhhhh! There it was, the only thing better than the smell of the books—books *plus* Dad's freshly-baked chocolate chip cookies for his "guests." The guests are actually customers, but he says calling them "guests" feels more personal and friendly.

When I opened my eyes, I spotted the ever-present coffee pot sitting next to the plate stacked full of cookies in the nook along the back wall. The coffee added its own aroma to the mix. When he first opened the store, Dad added an oven, sink, and refrigerator to the staff room so he could always have fresh, warm, gooey, yummy, chocolatey cookies available for his guests. And, of course, right next to those gooey cookies, he has napkins, hand-wipes, and a funny sign asking people to clean up before going near the books:

Eat a cookie, have a few. Please wipe your hands if you do!

Ari, Ellie, and I made a beeline to the treat table.

In addition to the chocolate chip cookies was a separate tray of sugar cookies with different colors of sprinkles. We could tell they were made from the same cookie cutter because they were the exact same shape, triangles with a little stem on the top or the bottom, depending on which way you looked at it. The ones with green and red sprinkles were clearly meant to be Christmas trees. The ones with the blue sprinkles that looked like upside down trees were meant to be *dreidels*, the spinning tops we play with on Hanukkah. What a clever idea.

But even better than the tree and dreidel cookies was what we found on the tray sitting next to the cookie platter.

"Ooh! *Sufganiyot!*" Ellie crowed as she grabbed a napkin and picked up a small, white-powdery, mini jelly donut.

"Soupy-what?" asked a guy who was younger than Dad but definitely out of high school. He poured himself a cup of coffee. "Sorry, I don't mean to be nosy, but I couldn't help overhearing you. What did you just say?"

"*Soof-gah-nee-yote*," Ellie repeated a little slower, emphasizing each syllable.

"Huh. They look like jelly donuts," he replied, confused.

"Yeah, they are! Sufganiyot is the Hebrew word for donuts," Ari explained.

I added, "On Hanukkah it's a tradition to eat foods made in oil because the holiday is all about how the oil lasted for eight days. Donuts are made in oil."

The guy nodded.

"Interesting. Yeah, I'm a little familiar with the story." He took a couple sips of coffee. "Traditions are nice. My family's tradition is pretending to like my grandma's burnt gingerbread cookies every Christmas."

We giggled.

Ellie continued. "We eat donuts and other fried foods like potato pancakes. Those are called latkes."

"Sounds like a holiday I could really get into!" he said, helping himself to a donut. "Thanks for the info about the soup-bunny-oats, or whatever you called them."

Ellie laughed with her mouth stuffed full of donut as she tried to say, "Sufganiyot!" It came out more like "shmoopy-goat."

The guy gave her an amused and somewhat puzzled look.

She tried again. "Shoomf-Gandhi-Goat!" This made her crack up even harder. Her laughing caused a puff of white powdered sugar to come out of her mouth, decorating her shirt. The guy chuckled and gave her a thumbs-up as he walked away with his coffee and his donut. Ari ran after him with a napkin and came right back.

I reached for a red and green tree cookie and said, "Mom did say we should have a snack."

"She actually said a *healthy* snack," my sister corrected me, while cleaning up the powdered sugar from her shirt with a wet wipe.

"Well, none of us remembered to bring the applesauce. Besides, cookies must have some nutritional value, right?" I said, trying to convince us all. "Eggs and flour? Those are healthy. I'll stop after this one."

"Okay, one more. She'll be so mad if we don't eat dinner tonight." Ellie said, almost sounding like our mother herself.

"Yeah, one more," I agreed, "then let's finish up and go see what we can do to help out. That's why we're here after all. So far we've only helped clear out some of the treats!"

Ari and Ellie agreed that we should stop all the noshing and go help out in the store.

After just one more.

While we stood there snacking happily, I gazed around the room, soaking in all my favorite things about The Silver Lining, like how the shelves have all

the books lined up in straight, neat, colorful rows. I especially appreciate the way everything is organized and
labeled, and that with hardly any effort at all, you
could navigate your way from a section on astronomy
to one on desserts. Big cushy chairs all around the
store, tucked away between rows of shelves, practically
beg guests to plop down and dive into a book. Or two
or three.

The kids' section is bright and cheerful, with cut-
outs of life-size book characters. We have, over the
years, played some awesome games of hide-and-seek
behind those characters and under the small tables
when it's not too crowded. (Don't tell my dad!)

People come from all over town to The Silver Lining. Even with online shopping and ginormous big-box
stores in malls and shopping centers, Dad has managed to create something unique that people come
back to again and again. It makes me so proud that my
very own dad created all of this. I would love The Silver
Lining even if it didn't belong to our family. How cool
is it that it's ours?

I looked up and saw a Santa Claus with his reindeer
hanging from the ceiling, and strings of little dancing
dreidels with smiling cartoon faces.

Santa had his helpers, and Dad had his.

"Let's get started," I said, feeling all motivated. "We
came here to help. Let's do some helping."

Ari and Ellie snapped out of their happy, sugar-
filled daydreams. We each took a napkin from the
stack next to the cookies and wiped our hands. I could
hear Mom's voice in my head telling us to wipe them
well to make sure we didn't get any *schmutz* on the
books. (Schmutz means dirt or mess in Yiddish.)

Ari said, "I guess it's time to mind the salt." Both Ellie and I looked at him, confused.

"Huh?" Ellie said

"Like your dad said before. Time to get back to the salt minding," Ari said.

Both Ellie and I laughed. "Ah, gotcha!" I said. "'The expression is 'back to the salt mines.' But yeah, let's get to work!"

10

Knock, Knock, It's Judah

The store was hopping! Tons of people were milling around, looking at books, sitting and reading, or hanging out by the food table enjoying treats and coffee. Dad floated around with a genuine smile on his face, greeting shoppers, chatting with them, and checking in with Imani, Ashley, and Dennis—his employees—to make sure everything was running smoothly. I love watching Dad in action in his store. He's so happy going from person to person, like a bee drifting from one flower to the next. He truly loves connecting people with books they'll enjoy.

"I'm going over to the biography section," Ellie said. "I wonder if we have that new book about Corey McDonald yet."

Ugh. Not him again.

"I'm not sure how that's 'helping,'" I said to Ari as Ellie headed to the other side of the store. "She eats, sleeps, and breathes Corey McDoofus. I can't imagine there's anything in that book she doesn't already know."

"Yeah," Ari replied, "I don't get it."

"Me neither," I said as we both, at the same time, stuck out our tongues and made gagging faces. "I mean, seriously! The guy sings about garbage trucks and sno-cones. He has no talent. What's the deal?"

Ari shrugged and shook his head, looking just as

bewildered as I was.

We looked around, wondering where to start.

We wandered over to the big round table nearest the entrance. That's where Dad puts new books as well as books that are just right for the month or the season. Sometimes he features certain authors or themes. This time, the table, like the rest of the store, was decorated for winter, and had all sorts of books for each holiday celebration.

I took a look at the Hanukkah collection. There were a zillion picture books for little kids, with pictures and drawings of dreidels, latkes, and menorahs. And while there were tons of little kid books, there were only a few for older kids. One stood out: *Forty-Four Fun Facts About Hanukkah*. Not exactly the most clever title, but it grabbed my attention anyway. I wondered why they chose such a random number. *I mean, forty-four? What's up with that?* I thought.

I found myself doing the one thing I can't stand when other people do it: I started flipping through the pages. When I have a new book in my hands, I open it up a tiny bit, stick my nose right into the crease, and take a big whiff. My other favorite thing is opening the cover, even if it's a soft-cover book, and feeling the newness as the cover crinkles and cracks open for the first time. I can't stand it when people bend the cover back and fan the pages so that the next person who opens the book doesn't get the thrill of that new-book crackle. But there I was, guilty.

There were a surprising number of interesting facts in that book with the not-so-great title, like how any candle holder with multiple branches is called a menorah, but one that is special for Hanukkah is also called a *hanukkiyah*. (It's pronounced *ha-noo-kee-YAH*. More than one are called *hanukkiyot,* pronounced *ha-noo-kee-YOTE.*) I already knew that but it was cool to see it in a book. I also read that some people use olive oil instead of candles to light their hanukkiyah because that's how they lit the menorahs back in ancient times. In our house, we use bright-colored candles. I love watching them melt and drip and make rainbow puddles on the foil that we put underneath, which then harden into new, funky-shaped wax pieces as they cool.

Another fun fact: the main person in the story is Judah Maccabee. I already knew that too. What I didn't know is that "maccabee" means "hammer." That would be a cool nickname! It gave me an idea for a joke.

"Knock, knock," I said out of the blue.

Without even looking up from the Kwanzaa picture book he was leafing through, Ari answered, "Who's there?"

"Judah."

"Judah, who?"

"Judah Maccabee," I answered with a chuckle.

That was the punchline, which he clearly didn't get. He finally looked up from the book and asked, "Judah Maccabee who?"

I said it again. This time, I exaggerated the name *Maccabee* and pounded my fist in the air as if I was hammering something.

He looked at me like my head had turned into a latke.

"Don't you get it?" I said with a huge smile on my face, pleased with my own brilliance.

"Wait, that was the joke?"

"Yeah, Judah *Maccabee!*"

"No, I absolutely do not get it." He looked at me

with crinkled eyebrows, waiting for an explanation so he could move past this painful part of the knock-knock joke and either laugh or get back to his book.

"Judah *Maccabee*," I explained, "because his name means Judah the *hammer*! He's knocking like a hammer knocks!" I pounded the air again for emphasis.

Ari pointed at me and said, "That may be the joke that wins you an award."

"Really?" I asked, surprised. I thought it was good but not *that* good.

"Yes, an award for the all-time world's worst joke," Ari said, patting me on the shoulder. "That was truly the pits, my friend. The worst. Bottom of the heap. An absolute stink bomb!"

I wasn't insulted. If someone else talked to me that way it might hurt my feelings but Ari's my best friend. He was probably right. I mean, if you have to explain a joke, you know it's a dud.

"All right, all right," I said, "I'll keep working on it." Then I added, "We should probably go see what my dad wants us to do."

Ari agreed. We put the books we were looking at back where we found them, straightened up the rest of the table, and went to find Dad.

We spotted him in the travel section, holding a pile of books so big we couldn't even see his face. I knew it was him because I recognized his shoes, his favorite black high-tops.

I spoke directly to the pile of books, "What can we do to help, Dad?"

He rested the stack on the table in front of him and steadied it before stepping away. It reminded me of the game Jenga. I imagined wiggling a book from the bottom of the pile, trying to slide it out without knocking down the whole tower.

"You know what would be great?" Dad asked. "I'd love it if you could reshelve all these books that I have here." He pointed at the Jenga-like tower. "I picked them up from all over the store, and it'd be super helpful if you could put them all back in their proper places."

"I can't believe people don't put the books back where they belong," Ari said, sounding a little offended.

Dad waved his hand as if he was shooing a fly away. "Happens all the time."

"Okay, we're on it," I said.

Ari and I spread the books out on the table and sorted through them.

"Let's do it by section," I suggested. "I'll take mysteries, biographies, and cookbooks. I'll also bring these crossword and brain games books to the Puzzles, Games, and Toys section."

"Good idea," Ari said. He collected an enormous bunch of picture books and headed toward the kids' room. I made my way to Puzzles, Games, and Toys. I shelved the crosswords and started to straighten the section, which always gets disorganized, especially at this time of year. I moved a 1000-piece puzzle box that was in the wrong spot, reshelved some word-find books that had been left in a messy pile, and neatened-up a stack of board games.

Then something caught my eye. It was so shocking that my breath actually caught for a second, almost like a hiccup. I stood there dumbfounded and just stared.

No way!

11

Mr. Melvin Magnifico's Marvelous, Miraculous Magic Kit: Deluxe Edition

W*hy didn't he tell me he had this here?* I wondered, still blown away by what I was seeing. I reached out and held the box in my two hands, which were actually shaking. It was like holding something valuable and rare, like King Tut's treasures or a baseball signed by all the original Brooklyn Dodgers.

Here it was, in our family's store. I walked slowly to the nearest cushy chair, not taking my eyes off the precious item in my hands for fear that if I looked away it might vanish. I sat down and gazed at the box in awe. I ran my finger across the embossed words under the plastic wrap:

Mr. Melvin Magnifico's Marvelous, Miraculous Magic Kit: Deluxe Edition.

Hooo! I quietly whistled through my teeth. The deluxe edition! I couldn't believe it.

After months of searching for it online, it practically fell into my lap in my own father's store. I had found it before on plenty of websites but the price was so steep that there was no way I could ever afford to buy it with my own money. And none of the sets that I had seen were like this one. This was the primo, top of the line, best of the best, most difficult-tricks-included, deluxe edition.

I turned it over and read the bottom of the box. It had everything you could ever need to do some of the most complicated, amazing magic tricks in existence, including instructions for the Floating Stack of Coins trick. I'd been struggling with this trick for weeks, trying to figure it out on my own, and now I held the solution in my hands! I'd been dreaming of owning this collection for so long, and now, here it was. I looked for the price.

"EIGHTY-NINE DOLLARS?" I actually said out loud, without thinking about it. It wouldn't have surprised me if people were staring but I was so focused on this uncovered treasure that I didn't notice.

Holy smokes! I thought to myself. *I can't afford eighty-nine dollars. But then again, I can't afford to let this opportunity pass me by.*

I jumped up from my seat, tucked the box under my arm, and went to find Ari in the kids' section. I was surprised when I got there to find not only Ari, but our friend Ethan Meyerson from Shul School.

"Hey, Ethan! What are you doing here?" I asked.

"I'm with my mom this week, and she needed to run some errands." I knew what he meant. Ethan's parents are divorced so he switches houses every week.

"Couldn't you have stayed home with Becky?" Ari asked. "I wish I had an older brother or sister, so I wouldn't have to get dragged everywhere. Or worse, have a 'babysitter,'" he said, making air quotes.

"Yeah, but since you don't have an older sibling to stay home with, you get to be an honorary member of the Silver family," I said, gently elbowing him.

Ari smiled. "That's true."

"I definitely didn't want to stay home alone with

Becky," Ethan said with an overexaggerated shudder, referring to his older sister. "Plus, when I heard that Mom was planning to come here for some holiday gifts, I wanted to come along. I love this place!"

"That's really nice to hear," I said, waiting to see if Ethan was going to say something sarcastic next. He enjoys being the class clown at Shul School, and we never know when he's going to be serious or silly. That gets him into trouble sometimes. He's a good guy, but once in a while he goes too far to get a laugh.

I couldn't wait another second to tell Ari about my incredible find, but before I could say anything, he held a book up in front of my face. "Check this out!" It was the latest Maggie Schnozzledork graphic novel. "Remember when we used to read these in second grade? I still think they're hysterical. Look at this." He opened it to a page with a drawing of a chihuahua wearing a human-sized backpack and laughed.

"Yeah, she's funny," I said, only half-listening to what he was saying. "But wait'll you see what I found!"

"Okay," Ari said as he slid the book back into its spot on the shelf, looking a little disappointed that I wasn't as excited about his amazing discovery as he'd expected. Under normal circumstances, I, too, would have jumped at the opportunity to dive into a new Schnozzledork masterpiece, but this was urgent.

I didn't even have to say a word. I just held the Melvin Magnifico box in front of him. His jaw dropped practically to his belly button, and his eyebrows nearly flew off the top of his head.

"Whoa!" he exclaimed.

"What?" Ethan asked, not understanding what was going on.

Ari ignored Ethan, looked me in the eye, and asked

with the exact amount of surprise and awe that I would have expected from my best friend, "Isn't that the one you've been looking for?"

"Yep!" I answered proudly, as if I had made the box appear out of thin air by performing one of my magic tricks.

"What's the big deal? What's going on?" Ethan asked.

Ari totally understood how enormous this news was, and seemed not to even hear Ethan.

"So how does this work? If it's in your dad's store, does that mean that it's yours? Do you get to keep it?" Ari asked.

"That's what I need to figure out."

"Come on, you guys! Tell me what you're talking about. What's the big deal with this magic set?" Ethan implored.

I filled Ethan in on the situation. He nodded with understanding. "Oh, I get it. So you're not sure if you can take it or not?"

"Right," I answered. "On the one hand, it's not mine to open. On the other hand, my dad already paid for it when he bought it for the store, so I guess in a way, he, and therefore *we* as a family, do kind of own it. On the other hand—"

Ari cut me off.

"Hold on, that's three hands! How many do you have?"

"It's all part of the magic," I answered, and the three of us laughed. "Like I was saying, on the other hand, he could make a lot of money if he sells it." I passed the box to Ari and pointed at the price. Ari whistled in disbelief exactly as I had done before.

Ari said, "Well, the decision seems pretty obvious

to me. If you open the box and perform some tricks in the store, people will be amazed and they'll want to buy their own magic sets. You'll help sell them. *That's how you can help your dad, which is what we came here to do.*"

"That's brilliant! You totally have to do it!" Ethan cheered, jumping up and down with excitement. Then in typical troublemaker Ethan-ness he said, "Don't overthink it. Just do it. I mean, come on, if this is your dad's store and he owns everything in it, and you're his kid, then you own it too. It's already yours! If you ask me, you own everything in the store." He made a grand gesture with his arms like he was painting an invisible rainbow in the air. "Lucky you."

Deep down, I couldn't imagine that this was true, but at the same time I really, really wanted it to be.

"Once I open it, though, he probably won't be able to sell it," I considered out loud.

"How is that any different from people sitting down and opening up the books, cracking the bindings, and not keeping them fresh and new anymore?" Ari asked, gesturing toward all the people sitting and reading. "I know that drives you crazy, but your dad seems to be okay with it."

Ethan started chanting quietly, "Do it! Do it! Do it!"

That's the big difference between Ethan and me. I clown around in class too, but I always think through the consequences. Ethan does what he thinks will be funny and worries about the outcome later. He doesn't seem to mind getting into trouble in class, but I sure do.

Ari joined in with Ethan.

"Do it! Do it! Do it!"

I felt like they were pressuring me to open the box,

and I honestly wasn't sure if it was okay or not.

Ari said, "C'mon, do it. If nothing else, this will prove that you're a true Bravey Cat. Jumping off the playground set was nothing compared to this."

Ethan doesn't go to Alexander Martin Elementary School with us, and had never heard of the Bravey Cats. He briefly looked puzzled, then resumed chanting, "Do it! Do it! Do it!"

My brain whirled with conflicting thoughts. I didn't want to let my friends down, and I wanted to prove to myself that I could be a Bravey Cat. On the other hand, the magician in me didn't want to share the secrets, and if we sold a lot of kits then lots more people would know how to do the tricks. On the other, other hand, selling a bunch of kits would be good for Dad's business. Even still, I wasn't completely convinced that opening the box was the right thing to do. But in the end, after going back and forth about it for several minutes, it did seem like maybe it was a good idea after all.

Finally I decided. "Yeah, I'd actually be helping. I'd be advertising this incredible product." I pictured myself dazzling an audience and leaving them in awe, wondering how I made the magic happen. My friends were right. I *had* to open the box in order to help out in the store. It was my duty.

"You're right, I need to do this," I said with great confidence, and took the box back from Ari.

Just then, Ethan's mom called him over and told him it was time to go.

"Good luck with the show," he said, pointing at me as he walked away. "Let me know how it goes. Don't chicken out and disappoint me!" He walked away chanting "Do it! Do it! Do it!"

Ari turned to me and asked, "Should I keep working in this area or do you want me to help you figure out the tricks?"

"I don't need any help," I answered abruptly. A magician doesn't share their secrets, even with their best friend. "I'll go into the back room and learn a couple of the easier tricks. It shouldn't take too long. Once I'm ready, I'll come out and you can help gather people to watch my act. How does that sound?"

"Great," Ari replied as he pulled the Schnozzledork book off the shelf again. I put my hands on my hips pretending to be angry at him for slacking off.

"What are you doing? We just made fun of Ellie for going off to look for the Corey McFlurry book. Now you're chilling with the Schnozz? Am I the only one helping around here?"

"Okay, okay, I just need to see how this part ends and then I'll get to work. I promise." I watched him walk toward one of the cushy chairs in the kids' section, his face practically inside the book, not looking where he was going. It was kind of funny when he banged into one of the overstuffed arms before plopping down.

I wove my way through the maze of shelves and hustled into the break room before anyone could see me.

The break room is a small, cozy area in the back of the shop where Dad and his employees take their lunch and coffee breaks. It's decorated with posters of some of Dad's all-time favorite books. Some of the posters even have autographs on them from the authors themselves.

The break room is also the place where they make the cookies and store the coffee and all the other delicious treats, so I knew I had to be quick. Dennis might come in for more cookies, and I didn't want anyone to catch me in there opening the box. I wiped down the table with a rag that was by the sink, to make sure it was clean and not sticky. Then I carefully placed the box on the table.

I took a pair of scissors from the coffee can filled with supplies that sat on a shelf behind the table. I turned the box over so that the bottom was facing up. Like a surgeon with a scalpel, I carefully pierced the plastic wrapping that sealed the box.

Once again, a blizzard of conflicting emotions came over me. I felt guilty for opening the box without permission, but I also felt happy because I'd be helping Dad with my skills. I couldn't decide if I should keep going, but the plastic was no longer sealed tightly around the box. It definitely didn't look new anymore. *Nope, no turning back now,* I thought as I slipped my finger under the plastic and tore off the rest of the wrap.

Any guilt or doubts magically evaporated the moment I lifted the box cover. A thick paperback book inside held the secrets to all the tricks in the box. Best of all, there was a twenty-page section on how to master the Floating Stack of Coins trick. I nearly fainted, or as my Grandma Ruth would say, I nearly *plotzed*!

A colorful treasure trove of magic gear surrounded the book: interlocking metal rings, little blue cups stacked one inside the other, multicolored handkerchiefs, red foam balls, and even a small toy rabbit you could pull out of a hat. There were two decks of cards—one was a trick deck and the other was a regular deck of playing cards. My pulse quickened when I found the magician's outfit, which included a collapsing black magic hat, a velvety black cape, and a sleek, plastic, magic wand. It was all so perfect.

I reached in and lifted the black wand with the white tip, and held it in my hand. This was no cheap, hollow piece of plastic. It had some heft to it, like there was something inside. I shook it, but it didn't make any sound. I swooshed it around in the air, and it felt amazing, like I could truly perform magic with it. In my brain, I knew that it was nothing more than a mass-produced toy made for amusing and delighting an audience. But for a moment, I was Harry Potter in Ollivanders Wand Shop. I imagined myself on a flying broomstick, making potions, and casting spells. I quickly shook my head, though, because I had to get busy learning the tricks. I couldn't very well justify opening the expensive kit if I wasn't going to actually use it to help sell more of them.

I sat down and flipped through the thick book, looking for simple but impressive tricks I could master quickly without too much preparation or rehearsing. After a few minutes of careful consideration, I decided to do the interlocking rings, the disappearing coin, and an easy rope trick. I also noticed that the card trick I did for YaYa was in the book. I figured that if things went really well and I needed an encore, that one would be perfect.

I read the instructions for each trick twice to make sure I totally understood how they worked, and then I practiced each one several times. I focused on the easier tricks from the front of the book because they looked impressive and would certainly wow a crowd— the super-complicated ones in the back of the book would require a lot of practice and would have to wait for another time. Once I was confident that I could smoothly perform each trick without messing up, I was ready to entertain and astonish the customers. I could hear my Grandpa Jack's voice in my head saying, "They won't know what hit 'em!"

I pictured my dad noticing the crowd forming around me, then hearing the thunderous claps and cheers after each trick. Each round of applause would draw even more people to gather around. The folks in the back would be standing on their tiptoes and craning their necks to see what was going on in the middle of the circle. Maybe some customers would even slide the big cushy chairs over so they could stand on them to see above the heads of the mob of onlookers. Guests would grab Mr. Melvin boxes off the shelf until there were none left, customers arguing and pushing one another, reaching for the very last one. Dad, the eternal peacemaker, would calm the shoppers and make a list of names for those who weren't quick enough to snatch a box of their own. He'd take orders for everyone who wanted one, promising to have the kits available within a couple of days. And, of course, Dad would gaze at me with pride, grateful for the booming business I'd brought to his store.

I didn't realize how nervous I was until I became aware of my clammy hands. Although I'd been playing practical jokes on people—especially my sister—for years already, this magic stuff was new. It wasn't the same as a practical joke or even a knock-knock joke that might not go over so well. This was a little scary. I don't like messing up, and if for some reason I bombed out, I'd be absolutely mortified. But, as my Zayde Miller, my grandpa who lives in Florida, would say, "The show must go on!"

I took a deep breath, packed all the pieces back into the box, except for the costume and the wand, and exhaled as I prepared for stardom.

12

Joel the Incredible

I whooshed out of the back room with the magician's top hat on my head, the cape tied around my neck, and the box tucked under my arm. As I neared the kids' section, I walked a little faster, which made the cape lift up a bit from behind me. That made me feel stronger, more confident, and even powerful.

I spotted Ari showing the Schnozzledork book to a potential customer. He was sharing all of his favorite things about the series to this first-grader who I recognized from school. The kid was looking up at him with big, wide eyes as if Ari himself was a hero from the Schnozzledork series. The kid listened intently, hanging on to his every word, as Ari described the characters and the stories.

As soon as Ari stopped talking, the kid began asking a million questions, in rapid-fire succession.

"How long did it take you to read the first one? Have you read all thirty-six books? Which one was your favorite? Did you read any of them more than once? Who's your favorite bad guy? Do you think Schnozzledork is the author's real name? How many—"

The kid stopped his questioning mid-sentence when he spotted me in my whole magician get-up. His eyes got even wider than they'd been when he was listening to Ari. I thought he was going to *plotz*!

"Hey there, young man," I said to him, making my

voice sound deeper and much older. "Wanna see a magic trick?" He looked like he had just won a lifetime supply of passes to Splash World waterpark.

"Yeah!" he squealed in delight.

"Great! I'm going to do a little show in about five minutes in the Games and Puzzles section." I pointed at the location with my wand. "Is that your mom?" I asked, now pointing my wand in the direction of the woman standing a few feet away looking at picture books with a little girl I assumed was his sister.

"Yeah! That *is* my mom!" he answered, already mystified by my incredible powers. "How'd you know that?"

I tapped my hat with the wand. "Magic," I said with a wink and a sly smile. Out of the corner of my eye I saw Ari stifling a laugh. "Be sure to ask her to bring you to the magic show. Remember, it's starting in about five minutes." I held my hand up with my fingers separated to exaggerate the number five.

"I will!" he responded, practically out of breath. Ari and I watched him run straight to his mom with his hand in the air and his fingers spread out just like mine, yelling, "Mommy! Mommy! There's gonna be a magic show in five minutes! Over there! Let's go!"

Ari poked me with his elbow and said, "Good work. That kid's going to be a perfect audience member." As we headed over to the Games and Puzzles area, he asked, "So, are you going to use Coppy as your magician name?"

"Oh," I said, "I hadn't thought about a magician's name. I probably shouldn't go with Coppy since it sounds more like a police officer than a magician. Plus, that's my secret Bravey Cat name, for club-use only. I'd better think of something else fast!"

I scanned the room, trying to find something that would spark an idea. Nothing inspired me. "Ugh! I don't know. Do you have any ideas?" I asked Ari.

"How about Joel the Great?"

"Boring!" I replied. "Let's keep brainstorming while we set up for the show."

We moved a small side table that was sitting next to one of the cushy chairs over to the games area. I saw Ellie coming toward us just as I placed the rope, the rings, and a quarter on the table. She was hugging a hardcover book in her arms like a teddy bear.

"Found it!" she said triumphantly, shoving the book practically into my nose. On the cover was a humongous picture of a toothy, smiling, nauseating Corey McDonald.

"Great," I said, glancing back down at the supplies in front of me. I was wondering which trick to do first.

"What are you wearing?" she asked, finally looking away from the book and taking notice of my magician's outfit.

"I'm going to do a little magic show. Look what I found! The outfit comes with the kit." I showed her the Melvin Magnifico box cover.

"Whoa! You found it here in the store?"

"Yeah, can you believe it?" I asked. "I was searching high and low, and Dad had a bunch of them all along. I didn't even think to ask him. It never occurred to me that I'd find it in a bookstore, but it was right here with the games and puzzles. It comes with a big, thick book inside, so I guess it does make sense to be in a bookstore."

"Amazing!" she exclaimed. "Are you going to do that card trick you did for me?"

"Maybe. But I'm doing this to show off the kit, to

help Dad sell a few. I'm going to do tricks that use the props that come in the kit."

"Cool idea. Maybe I'll do something like that to help Dad. I can do a reading from this book, although, let's be honest, this cover sells itself, don't you think?" she asked, hugging the book again.

I didn't even bother answering. She wouldn't have liked what I had to say anyway.

"I don't know why, but I'm a little bit nervous," I said to Ari and Ellie.

"You're such a good magician," Ellie, the eternal cheerleader, said, coaxing me on. "I think you may even be my very favorite magician. You'll be great."

"Aw, thanks, Ellie," I said. "That's really nice of you. But then again, given your taste in entertainers," I said, pointing at the Corey McDonald book with the wand, "I'm not so sure that that's a compliment." She socked me playfully in the arm, kind of like how Mom did to Dad in the foyer earlier.

"You're a Bravey Cat. You've got this," Ari said, patting my shoulder. "Come on, let's get started. Do you want me to make an announcement or something?"

"Sure," I said. "But what are you going to do about my name?"

He looked up at the ceiling. Santa Claus and his reindeer dangled above our heads. "How about North Pole Joel?"

"Nah," I answered with a wave of my hand.

He started brainstorming random words that rhymed with my name. "Eggroll Joel? Rock 'n' Roll Joel?" Then his face lit up. "I got it! Joel the Troll!"

I started to protest but he was already putting his hands up around his mouth to make the announcement.

"Hear ye, hear ye! Come meet the world's best magician!" he bellowed for everyone to hear. Then he added, still bellowing, "Or at least a pretty good one!"

A few people chuckled as they headed our way. One guest stopped to watch while another smiled as she passed by. Ari continued. "Gather 'round for a magic show that will astonish and amaze you! Young and old, come see Joel..." I shot him an angry glare to warn him not to call me Joel the Troll.

"...the Incredible!"

Not particularly catchy, but certainly better than Joel the Troll or Eggroll Joel. I smiled at him as a thank you. A few more people came by to see what was going on.

"Attention friends and guests of The Silver Lining!" I began, my confidence coming back. *I can totally do this.* "Behold, as I take this ordinary twenty-five cent piece in my hand. I will now make it disappear, and it will find its way into one of your pockets. The lucky winner will get to keep the quarter."

The boy from the kids' section nudged his way right in front of me, still looking like this was the absolute, best day of his life. I scanned the scene and counted ten people in the audience, including Ellie, Ari, the kid, his mom and his sister. It wasn't the throngs I had imagined but it was a start.

I decided to go *way* beyond the basics of the trick as described in the book. As my Bubby Miller, my grandma in Florida, would say, my performance was full of *schtick* and *schmaltz* (that means it was sort of over-the-top and cheesy, but in a good way).

I waved my wand, took off the hat and tapped it with the wand, flipped the hat in the air, and then twirled it with my finger before replacing it on my head. Only then did I close my fist and open it to show that the quarter was gone.

There was polite applause, which drew a couple more people over to the show, including my dad. He looked amused and proud, exactly as I had envisioned.

"Uh oh, I seem to have lost my quarter!" I said, hamming it up big time, patting my pants pockets. "Did someone take my quarter?" I started pointing at the people in the audience. "Did you take it, sir?"

A jolly old man with a big white beard, who could have passed for Santa Claus himself had he been wearing a red outfit and black shiny boots, shook his head and chuckled. "Sorry, son, it wasn't me," he said as if he was a part of the act.

"How about you, ma'am?" I asked the first-grader's mother.

"I don't have it," she said with a lighthearted laugh, showing me her empty hands.

"Well, somebody must have it!" I said, hamming it up even more. "I'll tell you what, please check your pockets just to be sure."

I was lucky to have a cooperative audience. Everyone began feeling around in their pockets. I looked over at the kid. His face went pale and his jaw dropped. He looked at me as if he had just seen a ghost.

"What? I mean, how? I mean, I have it!" he said, completely bewildered. He pulled the quarter out of his pocket and held it up over his head to show everyone. "Here it is! Here it is!"

I put my hands on my hips and pretended to scold the young thief. "Hey, why'd you take my quarter?" I made a big, exaggerated wink to the audience.

"I, I, I, I didn't," he said, looking terrified. His eyes started to get watery, so I quickly said, "I'm joking! I'm joking!" Relief washed over his face. "I made the quarter jump from my hand to your pocket."

"But how?" he asked, getting excited again, once he realized that he wasn't in trouble.

"That's the trick. It's magic!" I replied, and took a well-deserved bow. The audience applauded. Then I turned to the kid and said, "You can keep the quarter." His face lit up brighter than the Christmas tree, the Hanukkah menorah, the kinara, and the Diwali diya pots sitting in the front window, combined.

I looked up and saw that Dad was clapping, but not with the excited enthusiasm I had expected. I noticed that his eyebrows were furrowed and his mouth formed more of a straight line than a smile. I wasn't sure why, but figured that he had a lot on his mind. It was, after all, a busy shopping day. Or maybe he was trying to figure out how I did the trick. I couldn't tell, but the show had to go on.

I successfully performed the rope trick as well as the interlocking rings trick. By the time I finished, I silently counted thirteen people standing around me applauding, smiling, and chattering away.

Ari put his hands around his mouth like he did earlier and announced, "Don't forget to check out Mr. Melvin Magnifico's Marvelous, Miraculous Magic Kit. This one is the deluxe edition! You can learn how to do all these tricks and many, many more. Plus it makes a great gift!"

Mr. Santa Claus man went over to the shelf to take a look. The first-grade kid pulled on his mom's sleeve. "Mom, can I get a Magnifico Magic set? Please? *Please?*" He took her hand and pulled her over to the shelf where the rest of the Melvin Magnifico boxes were displayed.

Ari and I grinned proudly at each other. I couldn't

wait to see how many kits I had sold for Dad. But speaking of Dad, I looked around for him, expecting him to leap over to me, brimming with appreciation and compliments. I was surprised to see that he had already walked off and was over by the cash registers. It was kind of a letdown. But before I could wallow in my disappointment, I got distracted by the first-grade kid's voice.

"*Please*, Mom?" he begged. "I promise I'll never ask for anything ever again! I'll make my bed, I won't fight with you about taking a bath, I'll even brush my teeth! Please!"

"I'm not spending this much money, Milo," she said in a calm voice. "I'm sorry. Maybe Santa will bring it for Christmas." She put the box she'd been holding back on the shelf.

I felt bad for First Grade Kid, who I now knew was named Milo. Then he started to cry.

"What if Santa doesn't know that that's what I want?" he wailed. His wailing turned into eardrum-piercing sobs. Then, like the siren of a firetruck as it moves farther away, Milo's cries and sobs faded as his mother led him toward the door and out onto the sidewalk.

"Well, now I feel terrible," I said to Ari.

"Who knows? Maybe Santa will come through for him," he said.

"Yeah, maybe," I said, full of doubt. I peered over at Santa Claus guy, who was still checking out the box, and fantasized that he really was Santa, and that he would make Milo a happy boy.

My little performance had been a success, but I had a sinking feeling that it hadn't been such a great idea after all.

13

Don't Not Try

Everyone in our house has to help out at meal time, and it was my turn to set and clear the table. As I placed a plate in front of each seat, Mom said, "Don't bother setting a place for Dad. Remember? He's staying late at the store again. I'm probably going to run down there after dinner to help out tonight."

"Oh right, I forgot." I removed the plate I had just put down at Dad's spot, carried it back to the cupboard, and slid it back into the stack that remained.

"I guess that's both good news and bad news," Ellie said. "It's too bad he won't be home with us for dinner but he must be so busy that he has to stay late. That's good news for the store."

"Yeah," I agreed, but I was also disappointed that I'd have to wait to find out how many kits we had sold thanks to my little show. Dad had been so busy in the store that I decided to wait until he got home to ask. Now I had to wait even longer.

Jeremy lifted the cover off of the big pot that was on the stove, stuck his nose in, and said, "In other good news, we're having spaghetti and meatballs for dinner." It's always about the food with Jeremy.

The four of us sat down to eat. I hated seeing Dad's place empty, but we all knew that in the long run it was probably good news, as Ellie had said.

"So how was it in the store today?" Mom asked,

twirling a few strands of spaghetti onto her fork.

"The place was packed!" Jeremy exclaimed.

"How would you know?" Ellie asked in an accusing tone. "You weren't even there!"

"Yeah, I was. Dad asked me to come and bring him his reading glasses. I showed up while Joel was doing his sad, little magic show. It was so embarrassing. I ducked out as quickly as I could."

"Magic show?" Mom asked, looking at me, confused but interested.

Excitement and pride once again coursed through my veins.

"Yeah, Mom, I did an *awesome* magic show today right in the middle of the Games and Puzzles section." I glared at Jeremy as I replaced the words *sad* and *little* with the word *awesome*. "I happened to come across a stack of Mr. Melvin Magnifico's Marvelous, Miraculous Magic Kits—"

"Deluxe edition!" Ellie added with more enthusiasm than I ever would have expected from her. It's not like it was a Corey McDonald Magic Kit.

Mom looked shocked. "Dad let you open up one of those kits? I'm surprised. Aren't they very expensive?"

Wait, she knew about the magic kits too? She knew Dad had them in the store? How come no one told me?

"Well, he didn't *let* me open it, I just did. I wanted to surprise him. I thought that if I demonstrated how amazing the kits are, people would want to buy them and he'd end up selling way more than if they were just sitting on the shelf."

Mom pursed her lips like she was trying to hold back the words that wanted to spew out of her mouth. She took a deep breath and asked, "And did they sell?"

"I don't know! I'm dying to find out," I said with a

huff. "I was hoping to hear tonight at dinner. Now I have to wait until Dad gets home, whenever that may be."

"Well," Mom said, wiping her mouth with a napkin, "I hope for your sake that he sold a bunch because I do not think he's going to be happy with you."

Uh oh.

"You really should have asked first," Mom continued. "Do you know how much those kits cost, Joel?" I could tell from the tone of her voice that she wasn't actually asking me for the price. She already knew.

"Eighty-nine dollars!" Ellie sang out. "Can you imagine if YoYo got a whole bunch of people to buy them? Dad'll be so happy."

"Yes," Mom answered, "and can you imagine how angry Dad will be if they didn't? It's not the end of the world, but now he has a very expensive magic kit that he can't sell."

I looked down at the two meatballs left sitting on my plate. Suddenly I wasn't hungry anymore. I was worried. What if my brilliant idea turned out to be a giant flop? What if Dad was furious with me?

I pushed the plate away.

"You done with that?" Jeremy asked, his fork stabbing the first meatball before I could even respond. I was starting to feel more and more queasy.

"Mom," I asked, my voice cracking a little, "can I go with you to the store when you go? I need to know if he's mad at me, and if he is, I want to apologize. I honestly thought I was doing a good thing. I thought I was helping."

It must have been clear to everyone that I was feeling pretty awful because even my brother, who never misses a chance to pick on me, left me alone. I appreciated that.

"I understand," Mom said gently, "but it's a school night and I think you should stay home and get ready for bed. I'll help him close up the store, and I'll talk to him first. That way, if he is upset, maybe I can clear things up a bit before the two of you talk it over. How does that sound?"

I nodded without saying anything. I stood up from my place and started collecting the dishes, but my brother, with his bottomless-pit-for-a-stomach, barked, "Hey! I'm not done yet!" And indeed, he was going strong with no sign of slowing down.

"I'm not done either!" Ellie objected. "We just got started!"

"Have a seat and relax," Mom said. "No one is ready for you to clear the table."

I slumped down in my seat, rested my head against my hand, and watched my family eat while my stomach did flips. Jeremy sucked up the long strands of spaghetti from the plate into his mouth like a vacuum cleaner.

I sat there silently and thought about what might happen when Dad came home. I had two different scenes playing out inside my head. In one version, Dad walked through the front door bursting with energy, giving me a huge hug, practically lifting me off the floor, thanking me for the great job I did. In the second version, Dad stomped in from the cold, grunted at me, and then scolded me for what I did wrong.

I wanted to cry while Jeremy slurped his spaghetti and Ellie babbled on and on about the Corey McDonald book. They all went about their business while I felt like I was falling apart.

I could tell it was going to be a long night.

By the time Dad came home a couple of hours later, I had already showered and was in my usual bedtime outfit—pajama bottoms and a long-sleeve T-shirt. It was pretty late when I heard the click of the key in the lock. I ran to the front door. Mom walked in first, shook her head at me, and shot me a look as if to say, *Beware! He is not ready to talk with you.*

I swallowed hard and watched Dad put his gloves into the pockets of his coat, hang his coat in the front hall closet, and wrap his scarf around the hanger. He slipped his shoes off of his feet and left them on the mat to dry.

"Hi, Dad," I said, hoping for the best.

"Hi, Joel," he mumbled, without so much as glancing at me. And just like in scene number two that I played in my head, Dad grunted and walked directly into his home office. He carefully closed the glass door behind him. Dad usually calls us by our family nicknames at home, so when he didn't call me YoYo, I knew for sure that he was upset. Beyond that, he never goes straight into his office when he comes home. And he *never* closes the door when he's in there unless he's on an important phone call and needs some privacy.

Oh, this was bad. I looked up at Mom. She walked over to me and quietly said, "He's mad at you for taking it upon yourself to open up the magic kit. That said, he did seem to understand what you were trying to do. He's also very tired from working all day, so let him have some time alone. Wait until he comes out of the office to talk to him."

I nodded, speechless, feeling the lump in my throat grow from the size of a gumball to what felt like a volleyball. Knowing that he was so disappointed in me felt as awful as I would if I brought home a report card full of Fs.

"I was just trying to help," I said, tears in my eyes.

"I know," Mom said, giving me a little peck on top of my head. "And he knows it too. It'll be fine. Give him some space now, you can talk to him later."

I wanted to get out of there and not have to look him in the eye when he came out of the office. I decided to go talk to Ellie and see if she had any ideas about how to smooth things over. I trudged up the stairs feeling like I had bricks tied to my feet.

I knocked on her bedroom door. "YaYa, can I come in?"

"Sure," she said.

I turned the knob but the door only opened about a half an inch. I pushed a little harder but it still wouldn't budge. Something was in the way.

"Hold on, hold on," she called from behind the door. Through the crack that was open I saw her run over and pick up a couple of wet-looking towels. Once they were out of the way, the door opened easily. She dumped the towels on the floor right next to the hamper that was by her closet.

"What's going on in here?" I asked, pointing to the growing pile of laundry that could've easily been put inside the hamper.

"Oh, I'm just cleaning up" she answered, which I found perplexing because her room was even messier than usual. "Come in." She gestured, inviting me to enter the scary black hole that is her room.

Being around all that clutter makes me nervous but I Bravey-Catted it and went in anyway. I stepped over a hairbrush, her school bag, her flute case, and a banana, probably the same one I had seen in there the night before, so she must have had a different one in her lunch that day. I pushed aside a stack of magazines and papers by her dresser to make a place to sit down. This was no easy task because most of her dresser drawers were wide open, like giant mouths ready to swallow up whatever came too close. I stuffed her T-shirts into the drawer they were hanging out of so I could close it. One by one, I slid each drawer shut so I could sit on the floor and lean against the dresser.

"What's up?" she asked, jumping backwards onto her unmade bed. She crisscrossed her legs like a pretzel and sat on top of the rumpled comforter.

"Dad's home."

That's all I needed to say. She knew exactly where I was going with this.

"Uh oh," she replied. "Is he mad?"

"Yeah, it looks that way."

"Did you explain why you opened the Mr. Magnifico kit? Maybe he doesn't realize you were trying to help," she offered.

"I didn't get that far yet but I think Mom did. When he got home he barely looked at me, and went right into his office."

"Ooh, that's bad."

"Yeah, I know! That's why I came up here. Any suggestions about what I should do next?"

She sat and thought for a minute, resting her chin in her hands. She squinted so hard I could barely see her eyeballs moving around the room. After a few minutes, her gaze landed on the life-size poster of her hero Corey Mc-You-Know-Who, and she sat straight up.

"Well," she said, "you have to talk to him."

"I have to talk to Corey McMuffin?" I asked half-joking. I'm pretty sure she talks to her Corey poster when no one else is around.

She shook her head.

"No, you ding-dong," she said, ignoring my billionth obnoxious name for him, "you have to talk to Dad! I only *wish* we could talk to Corey. That would be an absolute dream come true." She stared at the poster, twirling her hair around her finger.

"Yeah, that's kind of what I figured," I said, snapping her out of her daydream.

"You know what he always says, don't you?"

"Who, Dad?" I asked.

"No, Corey!"

"Um, 'He loves me like a sno-cone'?" I answered sarcastically, quoting the ridiculous lyrics of one of his biggest hits.

"No!" she said, sounding partly amused and partly insulted. She was probably impressed that I knew one of his songs but also mad that I mocked him, which is what I was going for.

"'I'm as sweet as a chocolate chip'?" I said, remembering one of his even more ridiculous songs.

"No!" she said, frowning at me.

"'He lights up like a Ferris wheel at night when he sees me'? 'He's crushing on me like a garbage truck'?" Honestly, he is the worst.

"No," she finally cut me off, "'don't not try.'"

I stared at her blankly. I knew this was yet another one of his dopey songs but I didn't get it. I took a stab at it anyway. "You mean, 'try'?" I asked.

"Huh?"

"Why does he say 'don't not try'? Why not just say 'try'?"

"Because that's not very poetic, is it? The line goes like this:

You want to give up, you say it won't fly
But give it a go, don't not try!"

"That's idiotic."

"No it's not!" She looked up at the poster with an almost apologetic look as if to say, *Don't mind my rude brother, he doesn't know what he's talking about.* If I didn't know any better, I'd think that she actually believed Corey was right there in the room with us. She looked back at me.

"You can't chicken out. You need to go talk to Dad. He'll probably be angry at first, and it will be hard, but you have to be brave and do it."

I let out a deep, loud sigh. I knew she was right.

"Yeah," I said wearily, "okay, thanks."

Yep, I need to be brave. Like a Bravey Cat. Like Judah Maccabee, Judah the Hammer.

"Knock, knock," I said.

"Who's there?" she asked, not the least bit surprised that I launched into a knock-knock joke out of the blue.

"Judah."

"Judah, who?"

"Judah Maccabee," I answered, and tiptoed over all the junk on her floor and walked out, leaving her completely confused.

14

A Very "Challenging" Conversation

I plopped down at the kitchen table and waited for Dad. I knew he'd eventually make his way into the kitchen. He always does, especially after a long day at the store. It felt like forever but when he did finally come out of his office, he sat down across from me, reached into the bowl of fruit that we always have sitting on the table, and picked out an orange. He looked at me for an uncomfortably long time while he peeled the orange. His stare made me feel like ice cream melting on a hot sidewalk. Finally, several centuries later, he spoke.

"That was a cool magic show you did today," he said.

I was shocked. My mood began to swell like a balloon being filled with helium.

"Thanks!" I answered excitedly. This was not at all the way I imagined the conversation would go. Maybe he really *was* just tired. "Did you like the coin—" He cut me off before I could say "trick."

"But do you understand why I'm unhappy with what you did?"

Aaaaaand *POP!* went my hopeful helium balloon.

"Yes," I croaked. "I'm sorry."

There was a long, uncomfortable pause as I waited for him to accept my apology. Finally, I couldn't take it any longer. It was time to be a Bravey Cat. I took a deep breath and looked Dad right back in the eye.

"But do you understand why I did what I did?"

Dad looked at me with big, surprised eyes but then silently nodded as he finished peeling the orange.

The awkwardness was killing me. Besides, acting brave and mighty was hard. I blurted out in a tone slightly whinier than I intended, "I only wanted to help!"

Dad nodded again, absorbing this information.

"I appreciate that you thought you were helping. But what upset me the most was that you took something that wasn't yours without asking. Didn't it occur to you to ask me first?" He popped an orange section into his mouth.

"Well, it did, but you were so busy. Plus, I wanted to surprise you." I paused and took another deep breath. If I was being truly honest, I suppose I could have told him that I was just dying to open up the kit, and that a small part of me was secretly hoping I'd get to keep it. But I didn't say any of that out loud. Instead, I continued.

"I was so excited when I discovered that you had the Melvin kits in the store. I had no idea! And I knew that I'd be able to show it off for you. I thought that if I put on a show with the awesome magic kit, we'd sell a whole bunch. I'm very sorry I didn't ask you first." I paused again while Dad sat there, eating another section of orange. I added, "Just so you know, I did talk about it with Ari and Ethan Meyerson, who happened to be at the store too, and they both thought it would be a good idea to open the box and do the show."

Dad said gently, "It's nice that you have good friends you can talk to, but this only reinforces to me that you need to do a better job of making your own decisions and figuring out what's right or wrong. Don't let others pressure you into doing something you're not comfortable doing." He silently offered me a piece of orange. I took it even though I had already brushed my teeth. It felt like a peace offering of sorts, and I didn't want to come across as not wanting to make up with him.

"They didn't pressure me," I said, defending my friends. The truth of the matter is that I did feel pressured by them to open the kit, but I didn't want to get either of them in trouble. "They agreed that it would be a great idea to do the show. It was totally my idea. I mean, yeah, they encouraged me, but they never *forced* me to do anything. Plus, I kind of figured that it's not so different from how people open up the books and read them in the store, making them not-exactly-brand-new anymore. That's why I thought it would be okay for me to open the box."

"Okay," Dad said slowly, "so the two things you need to take away from this conversation are that you should never take something that doesn't belong to you unless you have permission from the owner, and that you need to make good choices. If you think something could possibly be a bad idea or have a negative outcome, then really think it through and consider the consequences before you do anything. If you're not sure, it's always good to ask. And for sure, don't let anyone talk you into doing something you don't feel comfortable doing."

"I did ask! I asked my friends. I promise you, we

talked about it, but I made the final decision." I most definitely did not want Dad to go and call Ari's or Ethan's parents and get them in trouble.

I stopped and considered Dad's comment about being pressured into doing something. I wondered if that was going to be a problem in our Bravey Cats club. I had a feeling that there would be some things I wouldn't want to do. I'm definitely not the bravest cat around.

I'm also not a nail biter, but thinking about the club and the challenges that might come up made me feel anxious. Before I knew it, my fingernail was in my mouth and I was biting it, trying to snag off a piece between my front teeth.

I messed up, and it was stressing me out. Big, heavy teardrops welled up in my eye sockets, and then rolled down my cheeks. I wiped my face with my sleeve. Dad looked at me and stretched his arms out like a bird with a huge wingspan and said, "Come here."

I stood up and rested my head against Dad's shoulder. He wrapped his arms around me for a long, tight hug. Then he held me out at arm's length and said, "I get what you were trying to do, and I sincerely thank you for wanting to help. But in the future, please ask before you take something that doesn't belong to you. Okay?"

This time it was my turn to nod silently, as I dabbed the last of my tears on my sleeve.

After the clock on the kitchen wall ticked for several seconds, I finally asked what I'd been dying to know.

"So, did you sell any kits after I did the magic show?"

Dad looked sternly at me. A million thoughts ran through my head. What was he thinking?

"We sold one," he said softly. "I don't know if it had anything to do with your magic show, because I don't know what time it sold, but yes, when I did a quick review of today's sales before I left for home, I saw that we did, in fact, sell one Mr. Magnifico kit."

"For real? That's great! That's so exciting! So why are you mad at me? You should be happy!"

"Well, we sold one. I'm not excited like you are, but I'm also not mad. I'm just wiped out. This time of the year is both wonderful and exhausting. I'm in the store for so many hours that by the time I get home, I can't see straight. I'm sorry if I worried you. I was upset but I'm not mad. I appreciate and understand what you did, but I want you to recognize that it was basically stealing, even if your heart was in the right place."

The word stung me like a bee. My face got red and hot.

"Stealing? It wasn't stealing! The box never left the store!"

Dad said quietly, "Stealing means you're taking something that belongs to someone else without their permission, and stealing of any sort is absolutely never okay."

He didn't need to tell me that. Of course I knew that stealing is bad. I stood there absorbing what he had said.

Dad waited for me to reply. When the silence continued, he said, "Do you understand? Stealing is never an appropriate option. It's never okay."

"Yes it is," I said, hoping to lighten the mood.

"No," Dad said firmly, raising his voice a bit, "it isn't."

"It is in baseball! You've cheered me on for stealing bases in the past. It's part of the game!" I pointed my two index fingers at him and shot him a *Ha! I gotcha* look.

"Ah," Dad said with a tired but hearty chuckle, "you got me there." After a moment's pause he said, "Are we clear?"

"Yeah," I assured him. "I didn't think of opening the box as stealing, but I see what you're saying now."

"Good. I'm glad to hear that."

I was thinking that was the end of it. We had our little talk, and I understood that what I'd done was wrong and why he was upset with me. I even ate the second piece of orange he handed me. I was ready to move on. But Dad wasn't.

"I'm seeing this as a teachable moment," he began.

Oh brother, I thought to myself, *here we go with one of his "teachable moments."* Both of my parents do this. I understand why, and I'm usually okay with it in the end, but I always get a little bit sweaty in my palms when they announce that we're diving into a teachable moment.

"While I accept your apology, and appreciate that you may have convinced a customer to buy a magic set, I would like you to come to The Silver Lining during your free time for the next two weeks to make up for your mistake. It's going to get busier and busier in the store. You can straighten out and restock the shelves, help customers—"

"You mean 'guests,' don't you, Dad?"

"Yes, yes, yes. You can help the guests. You can even help Dennis keep the cookie tray full."

"What about my homework? And Shul School? And basketball?" I asked, my voice cracking a little with worry.

"Of course those things will come first. But if you're

not at basketball or Shul School, and once you've finished your homework, I want you to come to the store. Agreed?" he asked, as if my opinion had anything to do with what was going to happen.

"Okay," I answered. "That's fair." Then, with a little hesitation I asked, "So now that the kit is already opened, do you think I can do my magic show when I'm at the store? Maybe we can sell even more of them." He stared blankly at me through his very tired, very heavy eyes, but I kept going, feeling more and more energized the more I thought about it. "And I only did the easy, simple tricks from the front of the book. The more I practice and try the harder tricks, the more spectacular my show will be, and everyone will want to buy Mr. Melvin kits! What do you think of that?"

Dad scratched his whiskers, which always appear after a long day. I noticed a couple of white ones, which surprised me.

"Sure," he finally said. "I don't see why not."

"Deal!" I exclaimed, putting my hand out for Dad to shake.

He shook my hand and then looked at me with a little smirk and asked, "So, can you tell me how you got the quarter into that kid's pocket?"

"Sorry, Dad, but a magician never reveals his secrets."

"Not even for your very own father?" he asked with a wink.

"Sorry, not gonna happen," I said, smiling at him.

"How about for your employer?" he asked with an even bigger grin.

I shook my head no.

"Fine," he said, giving in. "Can you at least do another trick for me?"

"Of course!" I said, thrilled to have an enthusiastic audience, even if it was a very tired audience of one.

I ran to get my deck of cards, and did the Jumping Aces trick for him.

"Hey, that's great!" he said when I pulled his card out of the deck. "All right, it's been a long day and it's getting quite late. Time for bed."

"Okay," I replied. "And thanks, Dad. I promise I won't take anything that isn't mine again without permission. I'll make better decisions in the future."

And honestly, I really did mean it.

15

Holy Bananas! What Did You Do?

It was the following Wednesday when things started to get out of hand.

Since it wasn't a Monday or a Friday, the Bravey Cats were not having an official lunch meeting, but like most other days, I sat at a table with my usual crew.

"Hey," I suggested to the group, "since we're together, let's practice using our nicknames even though this isn't an actual club meeting."

"Are we allowed to do that?" Patrick asked.

"I'm the nickname guy, I get to decide. Or would you rather vote on it?"

Brady said, "All in favor of using nicknames today, say 'Eyeball.'"

Everyone said "Eyeball" except for Micah, who shouted, "Eyelash!"

We all laughed, and then I continued. "Obviously, I don't have name tags for everyone today, so let's go around and reintroduce ourselves with our nicknames."

"Good idea. I can barely remember my own nickname," Brady said with a laugh and a mouthful of macaroni and cheese.

"You got the easy one!" Armando said. "At least your name and your nickname sound the same. If I ever stop eating string cheese my name won't make any sense at all." He held up his three string cheese sticks for us to see.

I got things rolling. "I'm Coppy," I said. I decided to explain my name even though absolutely no one asked about it. "I've gotten into doing magic lately, and David Copperfield is an amazing magician who has sort of become my idol. Coppy is from Copperfield."

Everyone nodded to show they got it. I'm still not sure they cared but I wanted them to know.

"Okay, who's next?" I asked. I took a bite of my sandwich now that I got the conversation started.

Brady said, "I'll go. I was just kidding before. I know my nickname. It's Brainy." He pointed at his head with his spoon, which still had some cheese on it from his mac and cheese, and got a little bit in his hair.

Ari said with an eye-roll, "I'm Archie," and continued eating his pizza bagel from home, which may have started out hot in the morning but looked cold and gross as he bit into it.

Micah said, "I'm Salty. You can remember it because my last name is Salzman, so it kind of sounds like Salty. Also, sometimes my mom says that I have a salty personality, but I don't even know what that means." Then he turned to me and said, "She thought it was kind of funny that you gave me that name when I told her."

"Hey!" Morgan said loudly, shooting Salty a look. "I thought the nicknames were like a secret, only to be used when we're together!"

"Oops!" Salty covered his mouth, embarrassed. "I guess I messed up. I won't tell anyone else."

"I'm Tricky," Patrick said, getting us back on track. Then he got up. Since he's one of the tallest kids in our grade and has that bright reddish-orange hair, he always seems to stand out in a crowd, even without standing up.

"There's a trick to remembering my name, but the trick isn't tricky." Then, much to our surprise, and fairly out of character for our smart, sensitive, sort of quiet friend, he started freestyling.

> *It's not because my personality is* elecTRIC
> *I'm not trying to be* egocenTRIC
> *or measure anything with* meTRICs
> *There you go, three words to help you, like a hat trick*
> *Now you'll remember I'm Tricky because my name is* Pa-TRICK!

We couldn't help ourselves. We all applauded his performance as he sat down and gave a humble bow with his head. Everyone around the room looked over at our table, probably curious to see what we were clapping about.

Morgan looked astonished. "Did you just make that up right now?"

Tricky nodded, a bit red-faced. He took a swig from the tiny red milk carton that came with his school lunch.

"Impressive! Well, I can't top that so I'll just share my name. I'm Buzzy. If you can't remember, just look at my head. Well, my hair, anyway."

Armando tossed back his longish brown hair, held up the one remaining string cheese that he hadn't yet eaten, and said, "You know what my name is!"

Last but not least came Demetrius, who stayed seated, for obvious reasons. "I'm Meat," he said. Then he pointed at his crutches, which were leaning up against the end of the table, and he introduced them too. "And these are the Crutchy Twins!"

We all laughed.

Archie couldn't wait to tell the group about what happened at The Silver Lining.

"You won't believe what Coppy did at his dad's bookstore yesterday." Everyone settled down and turned toward him. "He was such a Bravey Cat! He opened this awesome magic kit that he's had his eye on forever. Problem is, it's super expensive. He wasn't sure if he should open it, but he did, and then he put on this amazing magic show even though he was really nervous about it," Archie told the group. "Plus, there was a first-grader from our school there, and he truly believed that Joel had magical powers!"

"Coppy," I corrected.

"Yeah, Coppy. Although when you performed you were Joel the Incredible. Anyway, the kid was super impressed. It was great!"

"Wow!" Tricky said.

"Cool!" Buzzy said.

All my friends congratulated me on being a Bravey Cat. I'm not gonna lie, it felt pretty good to hear them say nice things to and about me. I didn't bother telling them that Dad scolded me about opening something that wasn't mine without asking first. I also didn't say anything about promising that I'd never do anything like that again.

"Hey, that gives me an idea," Brainy said excitedly. He was munching on an Oreo cookie and the chocolate covered all of his teeth. He looked like he only had gums in his mouth, so it was kind of hard to take him seriously. "So far we've had a couple of contests, but no real dares to prove our bravery. How about if we don't wait until Friday. Let's start now." This made me nervous. Given Brainy's not-so-great ideas up until now, I was worried about what he was going to say next.

"What about the girls?" Tricky asked. "Shouldn't we invite them over?"

"Nah," Brainy said, "these can be, like, unofficial practice dares. We'll count the real ones starting on Friday."

"Should we vote on it?" String Cheese asked.

"Well, if this isn't an official meeting and these aren't official dares, we can probably just do them for fun, not official business," Archie said. I thought the whole idea of us daring one another to do crazy stunts and calling it "business" was kind of funny. "So I vote that we shouldn't have to vote," he finished.

"All in favor of not voting, say 'Eyeball,'" Brainy said.

"Eyeball!" we shouted, and then laughed about the fact that we just voted to not vote.

"Okay, here's my dare for all of you sitting here," Brainy began. "I dare you to change something in one of your teacher's rooms. It has to be something that someone would notice, so you can't just do something easy like put a pencil on the floor."

"Okay, like what?" Buzzy asked.

"Uh," Brainy said, thinking for a moment, sniffling, as he often does. "Maybe switch around some of the things in the room. Move the globe from the front of the room to the back, or put the markers in the scissors bin."

"How about taping fake mustaches on all the posters in Mr. Foss's room?" Archie suggested.

We all laughed at that. Mr. Foss is our music teacher, and he has posters of famous musicians plastered all over the walls of his room. Some of them are men who already have mustaches, like Johann Strauss and Lin-Manuel Miranda, but he also has pictures of famous women musicians like Ella Fitzgerald and Dolly Parton, who definitely would look funny with mustaches. Much to my sister's delight—but certainly not to mine—he even has a picture of Corey McDonald on the wall. It's only there because Ellie and her friends donated it to the classroom. I wonder if Mr. Foss has ever even heard any of his songs. I think not, because if he had, he'd realize that McBarf-face doesn't begin to qualify as a musician.

The ideas kept coming. "How about rearranging the textbooks on the shelves so they're all facing backwards?" Meat offered.

"Maybe we could hide the pencil sharpener," Buzzy suggested.

"Or we could hide something *in* the pencil sharpener," String Cheese said.

"Well, we don't want to break anything. If we put something in the sharpener and someone goes to use it and it breaks the whole thing, that would be really bad," I said.

Everyone agreed.

We spent the rest of the lunch period coming up with funny and silly things we could do for our dares. I had to hand it to Brainy. This was actually a decent idea.

When lunch was over, Salty and I walked out of the lunchroom together.

"You know, Brady said—" I cut him off.

"Brainy!" I corrected him.

"Right, right, right," he said, not seeming too annoyed with my interruption. "Brainy only said it had to be a classroom. He didn't say which classroom or where. I bet Rabbi Green would think a little prank like this would be funny. He has a great sense of humor."

I agreed. "That's a great idea. He'd probably get a kick out of it, assuming we don't do anything too drastic. I'll try to come up with something. Let's not tell Ellie or Ari. We'll surprise them too."

"Ellie or *Archie*." This time it was his turn to correct me. "By the way, you really need to come up with a nickname for your sister and Asha and Megan."

"Yeah, I know," I replied.

And we left it at that.

Later that same day, just as she does every Wednesday, Mom picked us up after school to drive us to Shul School, which is at our synagogue. Jeremy was already sitting in the front next to Mom, so Ellie and I slid into the back seat when she pulled up. She handed us each a small container filled with—what else?—applesauce.

I've heard of kids at other synagogues who dread having to go to Hebrew school, but I love it. I look forward to going every Wednesday and Sunday. So does Ellie, and I'm pretty sure that even Jeremy likes it. (I have no doubt that if he didn't like it, he'd let us know.)

Another bonus of going to Shul School is that we get to hang out with our friends who go to other schools during the week and who we probably wouldn't see otherwise. Aside from my sister, Ari and Micah are my only two school friends who also go to Shul School with me. The three of us agreed that we wouldn't use our nicknames at Shul School, even if we were alone. It just didn't feel right.

There's also a girl named Hannah Glick who goes to Alexander Martin Elementary with us. We call her Know-It-All-Hannah but I wouldn't call her a friend. I have an easier time avoiding her at school, unlike at

Shul School, where our class is small. It's funny because we actually have a lot in common, and it almost seems like we should be friends. We're the first to raise our hands when the teacher asks a question. Not to be braggy or anything, but we're both pretty smart, and we get kind of competitive with one another. Not in a fun, friendly way, though.

Aside from having to see Hannah in class, I was looking forward to another lesson with Rabbi Green. He's the rabbi at our synagogue, but he's also the Shul School teacher for our grade.

Ohav Zedek is the name of the synagogue. It means "Love of Justice." When it comes to Rabbi Green's class, I'd call it "Ohav Kef," which means "Love of Fun." It's impossible to be bored in his class. For each new topic that he teaches us, he usually starts at least one of his lessons with a big surprise. It's often a funny entrance of some sort. Back in the fall, when we were learning about Rosh Hashanah, the Jewish New Year, Rabbi Green came into class and pulled the chair out from under his desk as if he was going to sit down. Instead, he stepped onto the chair and then all the way on top of his desk, where he blew a *shofar*, a ram's horn. It was wild! Then on *Sukkot*, the holiday that comes two weeks after Rosh Hashanah and celebrates the fall harvest, he shook himself as well as the *lulav* and *etrog*, the palm branch and lemon-like fruit we use for the holiday, while dancing and singing on top of the desk. It was hilarious.

As if reading my mind, Ellie turned to me and said, "Hanukkah starts next week already, and Rabbi Green still hasn't surprised us with a big entrance. I bet he'll do something today. What do you think it'll be?"

"I don't know," I said. "Maybe he'll come spinning

in like a dreidel?"

"Or maybe he'll give us all presents!" Ellie said with a laugh. "That would be nice."

Jeremy twisted his body from the front seat. "Yeah, that's likely," he said with a scowl, in his sarcastic, almost-a-teenager voice.

He turned back around to face the front, and Mom shook her head and snapped, "Jay!" and managed with only one word to communicate anger and disappointment, and make him feel guilty all in one shot. A classic Mom move!

When we got to the synagogue, Jeremy, as usual, jumped out of the front seat the instant the car came to a stop. He trotted off to find his friends while Ellie and I climbed out of the back seat and said goodbye to Mom in unison. We walked together into the synagogue. We usually have a few minutes when we get to Ohav Zedek to hang out with our friends before class begins. Ellie stopped to sit with her friends in the lobby. I looked down at my watch and saw that I had enough time to run to Rabbi Green's classroom, do my little prank, and join back up with my friends so we'd enter the room together. It worked like a charm. Rabbi Green wasn't there yet, so I did what I needed to do and returned to the lobby, where all the kids were hanging out.

When it was time to head to the classroom, we all shuffled through the long corridor to the building's education wing, talking up a storm, as always. Of course, Hannah had to be the first one to step foot in the classroom, and walked way ahead of the rest of us. When she got to the open doorway of Rabbi Green's class, she let out a scream so ear-shattering that it probably woke LuLu all the way across town in her bed in the kitchen.

"Hannah, chill!" Sydney Stern said, as she neared the classroom.

"Holy smokes, Hannah, what's your problem?" Matthew Steinberg asked, shaking his head.

"Hannah, you're acting like there's a dead body in our classroom!" said Mia Toledano, one of Ellie's Shul School besties.

As each kid arrived at the classroom, however, they too screamed. Before long, other kids from the nearby classrooms came running to see what was going on.

Micah turned to me and said, "Holy bananas, Joel! What did you do?"

16

Room in Ruins

The sixth-graders and seventh-graders pushed their way in to see for themselves what Hannah was screaming about. Being a lot shorter, I couldn't see past their shoulders. When I finally stepped into the classroom, I couldn't believe my eyes.

Mia screamed, "What happened in here?"

I looked around the room in disbelief and horror.

Papers were scattered all over the room. Everything that had been on the bulletin boards was lying all over the floor. Markers, pencils, and books were tossed about everywhere. All of Rabbi Green's desk drawers were open. A bunch of the kids' desks were lying on their sides—one was even all the way upside down with the legs sticking up in the air like a bug stuck on its back. Weirdest of all was the one-word message scrawled in capital letters across the whiteboard in red marker: "OBEY!"

Chaos had replaced Rabbi Green's normally neat and orderly room. It was almost as messy as my sister's bedroom. Almost.

Everyone stood in their places, surveying the damage. We were like statues, too shocked to move, until Hannah started picking things up off the floor.

"Don't touch anything!" Matthew yelled at her. "Don't disturb the crime scene! Wait until Rabbi Green gets here and sees it."

Micah turned to me once again and said, full of anger and shock, "Dude, what did you do? What were you thinking?"

"It wasn't me, I promise!"

Ari must have overheard the two of us so he came over. "You did this, Coppy? Why? Why on earth would you do this?"

"First of all, we're at Shul School, so no Bravey Cat names," I insisted.

"Fine," Ari said. "Why'd you do this, Joel? You're gonna be in so much trouble!"

"You're gonna be toast," Micah agreed.

"Second of all, I didn't do it. It wasn't me!" I insisted.

Micah pulled me by the sleeve out of the room and into the hallway. Ari followed. We had to walk a short distance so we could hear one another over the commotion coming out of the room.

"Weren't you pulling your prank before class today?" Micah asked.

"What prank? The dare Brainy—I mean Brady—suggested today?" Ari asked.

"Yeah," Micah answered. "Joel was going to change something in Rabbi Green's room. But I never expected anything like this!" He looked at me in a way that seemed both angry and maybe even hurt.

"I did sneak in before class, and I did the prank," I said. "But all I did was take the pictures that were on the front bulletin board and hang them upside down. It was funny. But you'd never know it now because everything's been torn down from the bulletin board. I don't understand. I was in this room only ten minutes ago, and it was totally fine. Come on, you know me, I would never destroy a classroom."

"That's true," Ari said.

Micah seemed satisfied too. It's true, I would never ever do anything like that, and they both certainly knew me well enough to know that.

Just then, Rabbi Green came down the hall, whistling the tune of the song "I Have a Little Dreidel."

My friends and I wanted to warn him. He was going to flip out when he saw what happened! But he seemed to not hear any of the noise coming from his room as he walked down the hallway with a bounce in his step.

"*Shalom, Micha, Yoel,* and *Ari,*" he said to us as if it was a perfectly normal day and he wasn't about to enter the scene of a massive crime. Rabbi Green always calls us by our Hebrew names. "Time for class! *Yala!* Let's go." He continued toward the room.

The three of us stared at one another in disbelief.

"What the heck is going on? Can't he hear the racket coming from his room?" Micah asked me.

"I have no idea!" I replied. We followed behind Rabbi Green.

The yelling and screaming stopped the moment he walked into the classroom. The room fell silent as everyone froze in place, waiting to see how Rabbi Green would react.

"Rabbi Green!" Hannah cried out, breaking the silence. "Someone's trashed your room!" She was practically in tears.

We expected him to go pale, to stand there with his eyes bugging out and his mouth open in shock, just as we had. Instead, he smiled at us and offered his usual cheery greeting of "*Shalom yeladim,*" which means, "Hello, children."

Morah Shira (Morah means teacher in Hebrew), who teaches sixth grade, and Mr. Pinsky, who teaches seventh grade, entered the room. It kind of made sense for them to join us because all the kids from their classes were already in there checking things out. But why was Mr. Pinsky—who is, like, a hundred years old—so calm? He wandered in slowly, like it was an ordinary day. Why wasn't Morah Shira texting for help? She's a college student, so of course she had her phone in her hand. Why weren't they weirded out like we were?

Rabbi Green casually looked around the room. Finally, he spoke.

"My goodness. What happened in here?" He was way too calm for the situation.

"It wasn't us!" Ethan cried out. "It was like this when we got here."

Everyone started yelling at once.

"Look at what they wrote on the board!"

"They knocked some desks over!"

"They went through your drawers!"

"The bulletin boards are all torn up!"

"They dumped out all of your markers and pencils and stuff!"

Rabbi Green nodded slowly as his eyes scanned the room.

"Well," he said quietly, "let's all start with cleaning up this mess. Sixth-graders and seventh-graders, you too. Everyone, please, let's put things back where they belong."

Matthew asked, "Shouldn't we leave things alone so that the investigators can examine the crime scene?"

Rabbi Green thought for a moment and then decided that we should go ahead and clean up after all.

Of course, we all did exactly as he asked. It didn't take long since there were so many of us in the room. We straightened out the desks and chairs, hung the pictures back on the bulletin boards, lined up all the books on the shelves, and gathered the markers and pencils and returned them to their proper places.

Matthew went to erase the creepy message on the board.

"Please leave that for now, *Matan*," Rabbi Green said.

Ari, Micah, and I all shared confused looks.

Once the room was back in order, Rabbi Green invited everyone, including the older kids, to sit down. I hadn't noticed it before, when the room was all messed up, but there were a whole bunch of extra chairs in the back of the room.

"Rabbi Green?" Mia asked. "What's going on? And why are the older kids staying in our room?"

I looked back to see Jeremy and his friends listening attentively, which was surprising. The seventh-graders have a reputation at Shul School for misbehaving, not paying attention to the teachers, and generally getting into trouble. I think they were just as confused and freaked out as the rest of us and wanted to know what was going on.

"First of all," Rabbi Green began, "thank you all for working as a team and doing such a speedy job of putting our classroom back together again. Yeladim, I want to hear from you how it felt to walk into our room and find it in such disarray. What were you thinking, what were you feeling? It must have been quite a shock."

"I was mad," Dahlia answered first. "How dare someone come in and destroy our classroom!"

"I felt kinda scared," one of the sixth-graders said. "Even though this isn't our classroom anymore, it's scary to think that anyone would do this here."

"Yeah, I felt scared and angry too," Ethan declared. "It felt creepy, like someone who didn't belong here had been in our room."

Rabbi Green listened and nodded with every comment.

My brother called out from the back of the room, pointing at the board in front, "What the heck does 'Obey' mean? I know what the word means but why would someone write that?"

"Yeah, that's what makes it so scary," Ilana Goldsmith, the girl sitting next to Jeremy who I think might be his secret girlfriend, said.

"Are you going to call the police?" Hannah asked. "I think it's obvious that we had an intruder in the building!"

The chatter in the room started up again as everyone began talking at once.

"Yeladim," Rabbi Green said at last, quieting everyone down. "Imagine for a moment that this isn't our classroom. Instead, imagine that we are the Jews living in Jerusalem at the time of the Hanukkah story. We've just returned to our Temple after the Greeks occupied it and destroyed it as they left. Perhaps you understand how they must have felt."

Ellie and I smiled at one another across the room. I mouthed to Ellie, *Big entrance!* Micah leaned over and whispered to me, "I get it now. Sorry I thought it was you who did this." I smiled to let him know it was fine.

"So you did all this?" one of the older kids asked.

"Guilty as charged," Rabbi Green said with a mischievous grin. "I apologize if I frightened you, that was not my intent. I just wanted you to experience what it must have felt like for the Jews to finally be able to re-enter the Temple only to find it in shambles. I bet you can now imagine some of the emotions they must have been feeling at the time."

"But what about the word 'Obey' on the board?" Jeremy asked again.

"Good question. Why do you think I put that there?" Rabbi Green tossed the question right back to my brother.

"I guess maybe that was what the Greeks were saying to the Jews?" he answered more as a question than a statement.

"*B'diyuk!* Exactly!" Rabbi Green exclaimed. "The Greeks tried to force the Jews to obey them, to follow their religious practices and way of life. It was a terrible time for the Jewish people. But just as we all worked together to put this room back into shape, that's exactly what the Jewish people did as they restored their beloved Temple. Then they rededicated the Temple, meaning that they made it holy and usable again, just as you did here."

Ethan interrupted. "I wouldn't exactly call this place holy." Some of us laughed.

Rabbi Green responded with a wink and said, "Isn't a place of learning always a holy place? In any case, you made it usable and presentable again, just as they did with the Temple. And that is why the holiday is called Hanukkah. *Hanukkah* is the Hebrew word for dedication or rededication."

Mia said, "I'm just relieved to know that someone didn't really come in here and destroy our classroom."

"Same here," I said.

"Me too," Ellie agreed. A chorus of "me too" echoed throughout the room.

"Again, I apologize for frightening some of you," Rabbi Green said. "I hope you understand what I was trying to do."

We all nodded to let him know that we got it.

"That was pretty intense, Rabbi Green," a seventh-grader named Michael said.

"Yes, I wanted to make an impression!" he said with a big smile. "Besides, you know how I enjoy making a spectacular entrance."

"We sure do," Matthew said.

"And now it's time for everyone to return to their own classrooms," Rabbi Green said. "Sixth-graders and seventh-graders, thank you for your concern and for your help."

"Aw!" the older kids whined as they got up and trudged out of the room with their teachers.

As they were walking out, Micah turned to me and said, "He sure tricked us!"

"I definitely love pranks," I replied, "but I can tell you for sure that I don't like being on the receiving end of one." I was still a little freaked out from the whole ordeal.

"Does this mean we should invite Rabbi Green to be a Bravey Cat? He pulled off quite the stunt," Micah joked.

"We may just have to!" I joked back.

17

Gift Rapping

O nce the room cleared out, Rabbi Green announced, "Time to talk about Hanukkah! Ready
to play Fast Facts?"

"Yeah!" we all yelled. We love the Fast Facts game.
The challenge is to review all we've learned in one minute or less. If Rabbi Green points at someone, that
person has to answer as quickly as possible. If he
doesn't point at someone, it's a free-for-all, and everyone can answer at once.

"Okay. Ready, set, go!" he said, and started the timer on his watch. "What was the name of the Greek ruler during the time of the Hanukkah story?" he asked
without pointing at anyone.

"Antiochus!" we shouted.

"What did he want the Jews to do?" He pointed at
Micah.

"He wanted all the Jews to live and act like the
Greeks," Micah blurted out.

"How did the Jews react to this?" He pointed at Abby.

"Some Jews gave up trying to be Jewish and took on
the Greek lifestyle, and others had to hide when doing
Jewish stuff."

"Name two things that the Jewish people had to
hide." He pointed at me.

"Keeping kosher and circumcising babies," I answered. A couple of the girls sitting behind me giggled. I rolled my eyes and tried to ignore them.

"Name one more thing the Jews weren't allowed to do." Jenna's turn.

"Study Torah!"

"What do some people say the Jews did when the Greek soldiers showed up unannounced, to hide that they were studying Torah?"

He didn't point. Another free-for-all.

"Play dreidel!"

"What's a dreidel?" he asked with a big smile on his face. He pointed at Ethan.

"The name of my cousin's dog!" he answered.

Rabbi Green laughed out loud, not expecting that answer. "*Eitan*, what else?"

When Ethan finally stopped laughing at his own cleverness, he gave the real answer. "It's a spinning top with letters on each of the four sides."

"Almost out of time," Rabbi Green said in a high-pitched voice. "Quickly, name the two rabbis who argued all the time."

He pointed at Sydney.

"Hillel and Shammai!" she answered at lightning speed.

He pointed at Mia. "Five seconds left! *Miriam*, tell us again the fun fact about Hillel and Shammai that you shared last week."

Mia opened her mouth to answer but Rabbi Green's timer beeped.

"Time's up!" he said. "Nice job, everyone."

Mia frowned. "Can I still answer the question?" she asked.

Rabbi Green consulted the class. "You all okay with that?"

Everyone nodded. She had already told us the story but it was cool enough that nobody objected.

"Thanks," she began. "So, Hillel and Shammai saw things very differently. Last summer on our trip to Israel, our tour guide took us to Hillel Street in Jerusalem. We walked one block over and there was Shammai Street. The guide explained that because Hillel and Shammai argued so much, when they named streets after them, they chose streets that were parallel and never meet up. Because the two sages could never agree or come together. Get it?"

Hannah jumped up and butted in, "Actually, Hillel and Shammai hardly ever argued with each other. It was their students who argued and disagreed. They were called Beit Hillel and Beit Shammai, which means the House of Hillel and the House of Shammai." She sat down with a proud look on her face.

Rabbi Green said, "Good catch, Chana, but how about for simplicity's sake we just refer to them as Hillel and Shammai?"

Hannah gave a thumbs-up to show her approval.

Rabbi Green went on. "Now I have to ask the follow-up question. What do Hillel and Shammai have to do with Hanukkah?"

I raised my hand and he pointed at me.

"One of Hillel and Shammai's most famous arguments was that Shammai said we should light all eight candles on the first night of Hanukkah and take one away each night, so as the holiday gets nearer to the end, so do the lights until they're all gone. Hillel argued that we should do it the opposite way, which is what we actually do now. We start with one candle on the first night and add a new one each night until our menorahs are blazing with so much fire on the eighth night that the whole room glows."

"*Yafeh me'od!* Very nice!" Rabbi Green said, smiling. "One last question. Who can tell me the important rule about the light we get from the hanukkiyah?"

My sister's hand shot up and he pointed at her.

"We're supposed to look at and enjoy the light but we aren't allowed to use it to read by or anything like that."

"*Nachon!* Correct!" Rabbi Green crowed. "You guys have been paying attention. Now let's move on to to-day's topic: Hanukkah gifts."

There was an explosion of whoops and cheers.

Okay, here it comes, I thought. *Maybe Ellie was right after all. Maybe he's going to give us all presents!*

"What are your thoughts on Hanukkah presents?" he asked.

"Presents are awesome!"

"That's the best part of Hanukkah!"

"You can never get too many of them!"

"We love them!" I shouted. I mean, come on, who doesn't?

Rabbi Green walked around the room as he spoke, making eye contact with each of us one at a time, with an almost mischievous gleam in his eye. "What would you say if I told you that, in my family, we don't buy gifts for each other on Hanukkah?" he asked.

"What?" Ari exclaimed.

"I would say that I feel bad for your kids!" Sydney shouted.

"Yeah, why would you be so mean? You're usually so nice!" Abby said in her typical loud voice.

"I promise, it's not to be mean. I'll tell you why," Rabbi Green began. "The tradition of giving gifts on Hanukkah is actually borrowed from the holiday of

Christmas. Gift-giving was never a big part of the holiday until the recent past. It was, however, a tradition for parents to give their children *gelt*," he explained.

"My parents give me guilt all year long!" Ethan joked.

"Not guilt," Rabbi Green said with a little laugh, "gelt, which is Yiddish for money."

"I thought gelt was those chocolate coins wrapped up in gold or silver foil," Jenna interrupted.

"Yes," Rabbi Green said as he whipped out a big bag of those very same chocolate coins from behind his back. It was almost like one of my magic tricks, the way he made it appear out of thin air. As he strolled around the room, he deposited a small pile of chocolate coins on each of our desks. *Now we're talking!*

"Today we give out chocolate gelt, but originally, parents gave their children coins as a Hanukkah gift. Go ahead and enjoy this gelt as we continue discussing."

Best. Teacher. Ever.

We tore into them, peeling off the metal foil and finding the yummy chocolate inside. I put the first piece of gelt between my front teeth and took a satisfying bite. It snapped in half, leaving me with the other half yet to eat. I watched some of the kids snarf their chocolate in one gulp as if it might disappear if they didn't eat it quickly enough. My plan was to savor it and make it last as long as possible.

Rabbi Green continued as we devoured our chocolate coins. "To tell you the truth, I loved getting presents when I was growing up. We only stopped buying gifts a couple of years ago."

"Why did you stop?" Mia asked.

"Well, it didn't seem right to me to follow a custom

that belongs to another religion when, in my mind, Hanukkah is all about *not* conforming, *not* borrowing other people's cultures. We've been discussing how, on Hanukkah, we remember the way the Jews fought for their rights to be Jewish and not have to take on the Greeks' way of life. So, why would we then take on someone else's practice? It seems to go against everything the Maccabees fought for."

I thought about that for a moment and realized that while it made sense, I didn't like it at all—not one bit! I always look forward to getting Hanukkah presents. It's one of my favorite things about the holiday, and it's way too much fun to give them up.

He went on. "At first, as you can probably guess, our kids were very upset." A bunch of us nodded to show we were on the same side as his kids, who are a little younger than us. "They agreed to it but, honestly, they weren't happy about giving up presents. After all, giving each other gifts did add a lot of joy and excitement to the holiday. And there really is something wonderful about giving gifts to those we love. So we decided to try a couple of different ways to celebrate that, for us, seemed to be more in line with the meaning of Hanukkah."

"What do you do now?" Ari asked.

"Good question. One of the things that's special about Hanukkah is that we add light to the darkness. Like this!" He turned his back to us so we could all see the menorah on his *kippah*. (That's the small round head covering that some Jewish people wear.) He surprised us when the candles lit up with little flashing lights!

The room filled with oohs and ahhs.

Rabbi Green continued.

"Hanukkah comes at the darkest time of the year. Look outside." He gestured toward the window. "It's not even five o'clock yet and it feels like nighttime already. On Hanukkah, as Hillel taught us, we add one more candle each night, adding a little more light to the world. So, in our family, instead of buying stuff, we create things that bring light and happiness to each other. For example, my wife, Rebecca, spent a whole day making a really special, fancy-shmancy gourmet dinner for us all last year. Our daughter, Tali, painted a picture that we framed and hung in our family room. Our other daughter, Noa, and I made hand-dipped candles to light on Hanukkah. This year I'm working on a rap that I'm going to sing to my family. Want to hear it?"

"Yeah!" we all screamed.

"Okay, if you insist," he said with his famous wink and smile. He pulled a piece of paper from his pants pocket, unfolded it, and shook it out. "I've been carrying this around all week. Here's what I have so far. Can someone give me a beat?"

Jenna put her hands up to her mouth and began making beatbox sounds.

"Niiiiice!" Rabbi Green exclaimed.

Coolest. Rabbi. Ever.

He cleared his throat, took a deep breath, and began.

> *On Hanukkah we light our lights*
> *We sing our songs for all eight nights*
>
> *We fry our dough and fry our taters*
> *We keep sour cream in our refrigerators*

We take our dreidels, make 'em spin
You have to pay if you get a shin

A great big miracle happened there
Candles in the window make our neighbors aware

We remember our hero Judah Mac
Don't eat too many latkes or you'll have a heart
attack.

He took a deep bow. A few kids, including Know-It-All-Hannah, of course, applauded.

"So, what do you guys think? Thumbs-up or thumbs-down?" Rabbi Green asked.

About a third of the class gave him a thumbs-up and almost everyone else gave him a thumbs-down. I couldn't lie, I thought it was kind of corny but also creative. I twisted my hand back and forth to show that I thought it was so-so.

"So bad," Jonah Segal said, shaking his head and laughing.

"I liked the taters and refrigerators line," Sydney said.

"I loved the whole thing," exclaimed Hannah, the only one still applauding.

"Don't quit your day job!" Ethan joked.

"Yeah, maybe I'll keep working on it," Rabbi Green said. "At least I'm having fun making it up. If nothing else, it'll make them all laugh, and laughter is always a great gift."

Mia said, "Rabbi Green, you mentioned that you do a couple of things with Hanukkah gifts. One is you make things for each other, but what else?"

"Oh, right, I got sidetracked with my rapping. The

second thing is, while we stopped buying presents for one another, we may still buy gifts for others in need. For example, last year, we bought some new toys for the children's hospital and delivered them on Hanukkah. Sometimes we give the gift of our time. This year we're planning to go play bingo with the folks at the Davidson Residence."

A few kids must have looked confused because he added, "That's the local Jewish home for the elderly." I knew that already. My great-grandma Pearl used to live there before she died.

Rabbi Green's whole face lit up. "Ooh! Maybe this year I'll share my rap with them! That'll entertain them!"

"You'd better make sure they don't have their hearing aids in," Matthew said. "They'll enjoy it much more that way!"

Rabbi Green laughed, waggling his finger at Matthew. "Hey now!" He has a great sense of humor. I don't think there's a single teacher at my "real" school that we could joke around with the way we do with Rabbi Green. Finally, he said to the class, "Anyway, back to what we were talking about, Even though we stopped buying gifts for each other in my house, I would never tell you that you shouldn't get gifts on Hanukkah if that's your family's *minhag*."

"What's a minhag?" Dahlia asked. "Sounds like a tiny, little pig. Like a mini-hog!"

He chuckled. "Cute, Dahlia. It does sound kind of like that. But the word minhag means custom, as in, how you celebrate. In other words if it's your family's custom to give gifts, by all means, I think that's wonderful. But I'm going to challenge you with something to think about. I'd like you to find something that you can do, or make, or bring to the world that will add light. The question is, what do you want to give?"

Hannah's hand sprung up. *Ugh, there she goes again.*

Rabbi Green said, "I don't need to hear your answers right now. This is a think-about-it question." He turned around, erased the word "OBEY!" from the whiteboard, and wrote in orange marker, *What gift will you give to others that will add light on Hanukkah?* Then he drew a cartoon smiley-faced menorah, kind of like the one on his kippah, with all the candles burning.

We sat there, quietly thinking. *I'm helping Dad at the store,* I thought. *It wasn't my choice, but that's something I'm already doing to help someone else.*

I popped an entire piece of gelt into my mouth and wondered how else to bring light into the world. The one thing I was sure of was that it wasn't going to involve rap.

18

Almost Like Magic

Things were pretty hectic. I guess that's what happens when you don't have any free time to lie around and be lazy or even just hang out with your best friend playing foosball and Battleship for hours. Every minute of every day was filled with school, chores, and homework; Shul School on Wednesdays and Sundays; basketball on Tuesdays and Thursdays. And, of course, whenever I wasn't doing any of that stuff, I was helping Dad and doing magic shows at The Silver Lining.

My only true free time was on *Shabbat*, which begins at sundown on Friday nights and goes through Saturday night. That's the Jewish Sabbath, our day off from work. In my family, we go to synagogue, relax, and just hang out on Shabbat. Other than that, the very rare pockets of time when I had nothing to do tended to happen at bedtime. That's when I'd reach under my bed, pull out the thick paperback instruction book that came with the Mr. Melvin Magnifico magic kit. I had borrowed the book from the store (with Dad's permission!) to study up on how to do the tougher tricks in the back of the book. Now that the box was opened and wasn't brand new anymore, Dad was keeping it in the back room for me to use for demonstrations. I'd been performing at the store and wanted to up my game.

I had originally figured I'd be able to do the Floating Stack of Coins trick with maybe just a bit of practice, no problem. As it turned out, that trick was impossible! I understood how to do it with one coin, but a stack of coins? No way!

The crazy thing is that when it's performed well it looks so incredibly easy that it almost doesn't seem like much of a trick at all. (Aside from involving a lack of gravity!) But believe me, once you try to do it, you realize that you practically need to be an all-powerful being who can defy the laws of physics and split the Red Sea or make a burning bush talk! Because there's no logical way that this trick should work.

I don't even know how much time I spent trying to get that stack of coins to levitate. Every night I climbed into bed and tried and tried to get it to work, ultimately giving up and shutting off the light. I'd lie there in the dark unable to sleep. Inevitably, my mind would wander to the Bravey Cats. Then, on top of being annoyed about my inability to do the trick, I'd worry about what sort of scary dares were looming on the horizon.

On the Thursday night before our Bravey Cat meeting, I almost got the trick to work for about half a second. Almost. As usual, after yet another failed attempt, I turned off the lamp by my bed and flipped over onto my side, feeling disappointment, annoyance, and worry all at once. It was not a good formula for falling asleep.

Then, all of a sudden, an idea popped into my head like a package magically showing up on my doorstep. I sat straight up in my bed, eyes wide open in the dark. I knew exactly what my dare was going to be for my Bravey Cats homework, and it didn't involve anything scary, dangerous, or destructive. I was going to, as Dad says, "kill two birds with one stone." (I never liked that particular Dad-ism, though, because I don't really ever want to kill any birds.) Luckily, the next day was Friday, which meant that we were having our meeting at lunchtime.

We gathered around our table in the lunchroom. Before we even got started, Megan asked me, "So, did you come up with club names for me, Asha, and Ellie?"

"Oops, I forgot," I admitted, embarrassed. Now I felt bad. "I'm sorry. I'll keep working on it."

She didn't seem to be too upset. In fact, it was Megan who started us off with our first challenge.

"Okay, I've got one!" She waved her soup spoon around. "Let's see who can get a spoon to stick to their nose the longest."

"Yeah, let's do that, but you're going to have to show us how," Tricky said.

"This'll be easy for you since you're so good at magic tricks," Ellie said to me.

"Well, first everyone needs a spoon," Megan said, laughing for having stated the obvious.

String Cheese stood up. "I'll go get some. Who else needs one?"

Five of us raised our hands. String Cheese raced to the front of the cafeteria and within seconds returned with the spoons.

Megan explained.

"OK, everyone, breathe hot air onto the inside part and then you just stick it on. It's that simple." She demonstrated how to do it, and with the spoon dangling from the tip of her nose, she slowly stretched her arms out and sang, "Tada!"

We all tried it. I couldn't get it to stay on at all. I looked at everyone at the table, and they all got the spoons to stay on their noses for a couple of seconds at least. I couldn't get it for even a nanosecond.

"Are you guys pranking me?" I asked. "Are you sticking it to your nose with gum or something?"

"No," Megan said with a giggle. To prove it to me, she removed the spoon from her nose and flashed it at me. "See, no gum." Then, in what seemed like an effort to show off, she breathed on it and put it back, making it dangle from the tip of her nose. She even moved her head slowly, side to side, while keeping the spoon in place for a couple of seconds before it fell off. It was almost like magic!

I kept on trying and was about to give up when I finally got it to stay for a moment. We were all laughing and making so much noise as the metal spoons kept falling and clanging on the table. Ms. Amato came over, and with a scowl told us to stop with all the clattering.

We promised we'd keep it down.

"What's Amato with her?" Meat joked. We all laughed.

Of course, we didn't stop trying to get our spoons to stick, but we made sure to catch them before they hit the table.

After a while we got tired of the spoon challenge and went back to eating. Nobody won that contest because the spoons kept falling off of all our noses. At least we had fun trying. I looked over at Megan and had an idea. I stood up, pointed my spoon at her and announced to the group, "Meet our newest club member, Spooner!"

"Hi, Spooner!" the group responded.

"One down, two to go," I said to Ellie and Asha. "I'm still working on names for the two of you. I'm sorry it's taking me so long but I want them to be just right." They didn't seem to mind.

While I was standing I said to the group, "I'd like to share my challenge now from the homework assignment we got the other day."

"Okay, go for it," Brainy replied.

"Great," I said. I pulled out some coins that I had tossed into my lunch bag that morning. "This is both a personal challenge for myself as well as for you all. I'm going to try to do a magic trick."

"I don't get it," Brainy interrupted. "How is that a challenge for us?"

"Let me explain," I said calmly. "I've been working on this trick for a long time, and the challenge for me is to actually get it right when I perform it for you. It's an incredibly difficult trick. I know what to do, but I haven't been able to master it."

I saw a lot of confused stares around the table.

"If you know me at all," I said, "you know that I can sometimes be pretty hard on myself. I'm a bit of a perfectionist that way. I don't like to mess up, so this is a big challenge for me to get it right."

"I still don't get how this is a challenge for our group," Brainy groaned.

"Well," I explained, "the challenge for me is to do it without messing up, and the challenge for you is that you have to figure out how I did it."

I had decided that it would be better to try and fail at a challenge I was comfortable with than to be faced with something that was too scary for me. Performing this trick was scary enough. I was kind of hoping to set an example so other club members would come up with cool challenges like mine rather than scary water slides or other terrifying activities.

"Great," Tricky mumbled through a forkful of potato salad. In fact, everyone looked like they thought this was a good idea.

Excellent, they're buying it! I thought to myself.

And with that, I started doing the trick. I didn't do all the schtick to make it a great show like I did in the bookstore, but I tried to make it entertaining by cracking jokes as I moved some pennies, nickels, and quarters around on the table.

"Hey, what do you get when you subtract a quarter from a quarter?" I waited a few seconds and then threw the punchline at them.

"Oh, never mind, that doesn't make any sense!"

They stared at me blankly. I held up the quarter and said, "It doesn't make any 'cents,' get it?"

More blank stares came at me from around the table.

"Twenty-five cents minus twenty-five cents leaves you without any cents!" They finally laughed, more to be polite than anything, it seemed. Okay, maybe it wasn't my best material.

Meanwhile, as I attempted to entertain them with humor, I could see their wide eyes and big smiles as I began stacking the coins. I was glad they were having fun but it also meant that they had high expectations.

Now, to see if I could pull it off.

19

Now You See 'Em, Now You Don't

Crash! The coins came tumbling down, clinking and clattering. It was definitely not the big finish I'd been working up to. My friends looked at me with a combination of disappointment and pity, while everyone else in the lunchroom turned around to see what the racket was all about. I really thought I was going to pull off the trick. I'm not sure why, since it had never worked at home, but I was kind of hoping that the pressure of performing would make it happen. I was embarrassed and mad at myself for even trying.

I got down on my hands and knees, and picked up the coins that had scattered and rolled all around the room. My friends joined me, and we looked like a pack of wolves sniffing out our prey as we moved along on the gross, sticky lunchroom floor.

Ms. Amato hurried over again to see what we were doing. *Man, she doesn't miss a thing!*

"Children!" she cried out. "What on earth are you doing down there?" Her shrieky voice hurt my ears.

"Oh, nothing," Buzzy said. "We dropped something but we're cleaning it up." I appreciated that Buzzy didn't blame it all on me.

"Almost done," I said, standing up, clutching the coins close to my belly.

"Very well then," she said. "Thank you for picking up after yourselves."

Once we collected everything we sat back at our table. YaYa, the one person in the world who knows me the very best and who can practically read my mind, put her hand on my shoulder and said in her ev-er-enthusiastic way, "I guess you picked a good challenge. If it was easy, it wouldn't be much of a challenge, right? Keep working on it, you'll get it."

"Yeah," Tricky agreed. "Plus, it'll probably be a super-hard challenge for us to figure it out."

All my friends nodded. *I do have good friends,* I thought to myself.

As we sat around the long table eating our lunches, we took turns sharing our ideas for challenges. Some felt very doable, like Archie's idea of trying to read a two-hundred-page book in one weekend. I liked that one. String Cheese dared us to sing like opera singers for one whole day, even in class. I worried that we might get in trouble but I also thought that one was pretty funny.

Other ideas were, as expected, freaky-scary, like El-lie's challenge of going down Dead Man's Drop at Splash World. Meat suggested that we try to sneak into the old abandoned railroad depot. I had absolutely no interest in doing that. That place creeps me out. Lots of kids say it's haunted but I don't believe it. I simply don't think we should be trespassing.

Brainy's idea was the absolute worst of all, and I was glad I wasn't the only one who thought so.

"I was walking on Walnut Street yesterday and passed a church that had a bunch of little statues of people and animals in a shed outside on the lawn," he began. "You know, it's that Christmas thing."

"You mean a nativity scene?" Meat asked.

"Yeah, I guess," Brainy said.

Archie asked, "What's a nativity scene?"

"It's a Christmas display that some people put in their yard," Buzzy explained. "It has statues of all the people in the story of when Jesus was born. There's baby Jesus, his parents Mary and Joseph, and the men who brought him gifts. Sometimes the scenes have angels and shepherds, and usually there are animals too. I mean, he was born in a stable, you know."

"Oh yeah, I've seen those around," Archie said. "My next door neighbors have a little one like that in their living room around Christmas time."

"So, anyway," Brainy continued, "I was walking along and I saw this one scene that had exactly eleven pieces, and I thought it would be a great prank if we each took one since there are eleven of us in the group now." He looked at us with a huge smile, apparently anticipating cheers and laughs for his brilliant idea. "Look, I even got us started!"

And that's when we lost it. Brainy had snuck a shopping bag with him into the lunchroom and had it sitting between his legs on the floor. He reached down and pulled out a statue of a sheep that was about as big as a lunch box. He plunked it in the middle of the table, beaming like a flashlight, waiting for us to shower him with compliments and applause.

Instead, we froze, like ten blocks of ice, dumbfounded, too shocked to speak. String Cheese broke the silence with a huge, roaring, furious, "WHAT DID YOU DO?"

And then we laid into him. Every single one of us screamed at him at the same time. I couldn't even tell who was saying what, but the entire lunchroom echoed with:

"WHAT'S WRONG WITH YOU?"

"ARE YOU CRAZY?"

"THAT'S SO DISRESPECTFUL!"

"I CAN'T BELIEVE YOU STOLE THAT!"

"YOU NEED TO RETURN THAT SHEEP IMMEDI-ATELY!"

Brainy cowered, covering his head with his arms as if we were pelting him with snowballs.

Ms. Amato returned to our table and, this time, yelled at us to keep it down. She didn't seem to notice the sheep sitting amongst us.

"Hey, it's just an idea," Brainy said defensively after she walked away. "It's not like we'd keep them, or anything. We'd take them for a day or two and then return them. We'd 'borrow' them—for the dare," he said. I couldn't believe he had the nerve to even try to defend his horrendous idea.

I had to say something.

"Brady." Yes, I used his real name because it was that serious. "Your idea is wrong on so many levels."

"*So* many levels," String Cheese repeated, shaking his head in disgust. The rest of the group did the same.

I continued.

"It's disrespectful and hurtful, not to mention that it's stealing." Dad's voice was in my head as I said, "And stealing means taking something that belongs to someone else without their permission. It's both wrong and illegal. We've come up with lots of good ideas for challenges but there is absolutely nothing good about this scheme of yours. If these are the kinds of challenges you have in mind for us, then I might have to drop out of the club."

"Not only that," String Cheese jumped in, "but the nativity scene is important to Christians. Taking the pieces is more than just mean and disrespectful, it's unholy."

"Yeah," Meat said. "I mean, come on, even if it's not part of your religion, it doesn't mean you shouldn't be respectful of it. It may not be important to you but it's important to someone."

Brainy's face changed from defensive and angry to apologetic as he wiped his nose on his sleeve.

"Okay, sorry," he said in a quiet voice. "I celebrate Christmas too but we don't do much of the religious stuff. We just do Santa and gifts and a big family dinner. I didn't realize that those were considered holy statues. I thought they were just decorations and that it would be funny. I thought you'd think so too."

"Holy or not holy, why would you want to steal something from someone?" Asha asked, looking shocked at the very thought of participating in such a prank. "I would never dream of taking anything from someone's yard—not a statue, not a toy that was left out overnight, not even a flower in somebody's garden."

"What in the world made you think this would be funny?" Spooner asked.

"Yeah," Ellie added, "which part of this was supposed to be funny?"

Brainy answered. "It wasn't like we were going to keep them. I thought it would be kind of funny if they magically disappeared and then magically reappeared. You know, 'now you see 'em, now you don't.' It'd be, like, a Christmas miracle. People would love it! The challenge for us would be to take them and put them back without getting caught, and since there were eleven of them and eleven of us, I thought it was perfect."

I was so angry. I thought about Dad and how he

gets disappointed and turns things into teachable moments. I tried, I really tried to be calmly disappointed like Dad rather than furious but I just couldn't do it. I couldn't believe that Brainy not only thought this was a good idea but thought that we'd like it. I hastily packed up my stuff and moved to a different table. Of course, my luck, the only open spot I could find was across from Know-It-All-Hannah. Fortunately, there were only a few minutes left in the lunch period. I sat down, avoiding Hannah's glare.

I had already finished eating and wanted to take my mind off of Brainy's bad idea, so I took out the coins and stacked them on the table, working on the trick again until the bell rang. Out of the corner of my eye I could feel Hannah watching me as she finished her lunch.

I was offended by Brainy's idea, frustrated about failing to perform the trick, I let Dad down, and now, to top it off, my least favorite classmate was practically breathing down my neck.

I was having a pretty tough day, feeling disappointed, sad, and angry. And wouldn't you know it, the moment the bell rang for us to leave the lunchroom, all of the coins came crashing down again.

20

We Like Rabbi Green a Latke!

Sunday morning came, and it was time to go back to Shul School. I met up with Ari and Micah in the lobby as usual. As we made our way to the classroom, I asked my buddies, "You don't think he's going to surprise us again, do you?"

"Not a chance," Ari said. "There's no way he could top his last big entrance. I'm sure his lesson will be fun—it always is—but there's no way he's going to even try to top that last class."

Micah agreed. "Yeah, plus he usually only does one big splashy entrance for each topic. Since we're in the middle of learning about Hanukkah, I'm pretty sure he's done with the surprises until the next holiday. That's the one with the trees, right?"

"You mean *Tu B'shvat*," I replied. "That's the one."

We all agreed that he was probably done with surprises for now. And yet, when it was time for class to begin, we eagerly watched the door to see how Rabbi Green would enter.

"I suppose he could come in dressed up for Hanukkah," Jonah said, joining us, having overheard our conversation. "I could see him making an entrance decked out in a full-body dreidel costume."

"Or dressed up like Judah Maccabee," I suggested hopefully. Even though I knew it was unlikely, I was still hoping for a fun start to class.

Rabbi Green was a few minutes late. When he finally arrived, he strolled in calmly, carrying a roll of paper towels tucked under his arm and a spray bottle of cleaning solution in his hand. No big entrance, no drama, no costumes. Even though he'd used up his big entrance quota for Hanukkah, it was disappointing nonetheless.

"Told ya," Ari said.

Rabbi Green waved at us, gave us a huge, warm smile, placed the two items on the right-hand edge of his desk, and walked right back out without saying a word. We all looked at one another, puzzled.

"What the heck is he up to?" I heard Dahlia ask Mia.

"Is he going to make us clean our desks? I've heard of cleaning for Passover but not for Hanukkah!" Abby said loudly.

We all waited to see what would happen next.

When Rabbi Green returned a few minutes later he was carrying a spatula, four spoons, and two soup bowls. He was balancing a box of forks on top of the bowls. In his other hand he held a huge jug of cooking oil. He put everything over to the side with the other things he had previously put down, and then once again, left without saying a word.

"Is he making soup?" Matthew asked, referring to the two bowls.

"He'd need more than two bowls if he was going to make soup for us," Mia replied. "Plus, look, he brought a box of forks and only four spoons."

"Latkes?" Ellie asked.

I was hoping that would be the case. I love latkes! Some people eat them all year long but they're really a Hanukkah food, kind of like how eggnog is a Christmas drink. You can have it anytime you want but having it only at holiday time makes it extra special. But what was the cleaning solution for?

"I *suppose* it could be latkes," Ari said hesitantly. I think he didn't want to get his hopes up.

A couple of minutes later Rabbi Green returned with yet another load of stuff. This time he had an electric skillet tucked under his left arm, with the cord hanging down like a tail, and a reusable grocery bag swinging from the crook of his right elbow. He placed the skillet on the desk near the other items, and plunked the bag down next to it. From the bag he pulled out two big jars of applesauce, a gigantic tub of sour cream, and a stack of paper plates. He tossed the empty bag into the corner and once again walked out of the room without saying anything. This time, though, he glanced sideways at us and gave us one of his familiar, sly, little smiles as he left.

"Latkes!" we all said to one another, this time with much more confidence.

Rabbi Green re-entered the room holding a big, shiny, silver mixing bowl. Just as we all hoped he would, he stepped onto his chair, then onto the cleared part of his desk—his signature move! He tilted the bowl toward us so we could see that it was filled with grayish-tan-colored mush. Then he lifted the large bowl over his head as if it was the Stanley Cup.

"LATKES!" he bellowed with the bowl in the air.

"LATKES!" we all repeated after him.

We cheered and applauded as Rabbi Green stepped down onto the chair and then the floor. He handed the bowl to Matthew, who was sitting up front, and asked him to hold onto it for a moment. Meanwhile, he sprayed the desk with the cleaning stuff and wiped down the area where he had been standing.

While rubbing circles with a paper towel on the desk, he finally greeted us with his usual cheery, "Shalom, yeladim!"

"Shalom, Rabbi Green," we all responded.

"Guess what we're doing in class today?" We all laughed, including Rabbi Green.

"Um, let me guess. Are we making latkes?" Dahlia asked sarcastically.

"Well, yes and no," he answered. "*I'm* going to make the latkes because I don't trust the sizzling, spitting hot oil with a room full of kids."

A chorus of voices let out a disappointed "Aww."

He continued. "You'll stay back at a safe distance. However, you will get to eat the latkes!" The class once again erupted in cheers. He motioned to Matthew to pass the bowl back to him, which he did.

"But of course, we aren't simply going to have a cooking class. Let's talk about why we eat latkes."

"Because Hanukkah is next week!" Abby shouted.

"Yes," Rabbi Green agreed, "but why latkes?"

"I know, I know!" Know-It-All-Hannah called out.

"Hold that thought, *Chana*," Rabbi Green said. "I want to quickly wash my hands before I start cooking." He jogged out of the room and was back in about a minute. In the meantime, Hannah sat there with her arm still in the air like someone had pushed the pause button on her. The second Rabbi Green stepped over the threshold of the classroom, Hannah blurted out her answer.

"It's because of the oil!" she said, pointing at the huge, industrial-sized jug that Rabbi Green must have gotten from the synagogue kitchen.

"Can you say more about that, *Chana*?" Rabbi

Green asked while pushing his desk with his butt all the way to the front wall, up against the whiteboard. He plugged the electric skillet into the outlet below and poured a bunch of oil into the pan.

Psyched to be the center of attention, Hannah repeated, "It's because of the oil. The Jewish people went into the Temple in Jerusalem that was destroyed and found one little container of oil, which was supposed to be enough to last for only one day. But then it lasted for eight. It was a miracle! So now we eat foods fried in oil to remember the miracle."

"Yeah," Ellie said, "we eat foods made in oil, like latkes and sufganiyot. I love this holiday!"

"My family also eats *sfenj*," Adam Fisher said. "My mom's family is from Morocco, so we do a lot of Sephardi customs. Sfenj is like sufganiyot, it's fried dough with sugar. It's so good!"

"We're Sephardi too and we also have sfenj in our house!" Mia said excitedly. "It's the best!"

My mouth started to water at the sound of that.

Rabbi Green smiled and said, "Good thing I'm cooking up some latkes. You're all making me very hungry. And *tov me'od*, very good, Chana. That is where the tradition comes from. Latkes are an Ashkenazi tradition from Eastern Europe the way sfenj is a Sephardi food from Morocco. Jews from all over the world enjoy different foods prepared in oil." Hannah's smile grew even broader, pleased with Rabbi Green's approval. "But what would you say if I told you that the legend of the oil isn't the most important part of the Hanukkah story?"

Hannah's smile drooped. She doesn't like being wrong and, to be honest, I understand because I don't either. Sometimes I feel bad for her because she tries so hard to get the teachers to like her, but most of the time I find her super irritating. Everyone does. Well, except for Rabbi Green, but that's because he's the rabbi. He has to like everyone.

"What do you mean, Rabbi Green?" Jenna asked. "I thought that was the whole story right there. The Temple gets destroyed, the Jews go in and light the menorah with enough oil for only one day, and it stays lit for eight days. That's it, short and sweet."

"It's not quite *that* short and sweet," he said. He took one of the large spoons, scooped up some of the tan-colored mush, and carefully placed it into the oil. The loud sizzle seemed to startle him, and he jumped back a bit. With his eyes fixed on the pan, he said, "That's definitely the tradition. But what if I told you that we're actually talking about an even greater miracle, which is really what we celebrate?"

Everyone in the room looked either fascinated or bewildered. A few kids squirmed in their seats. I mean, after all, this is the story we'd been hearing all of our lives. We'd always been taught that the miracle of Hanukkah is that the oil lasted for eight days. How could everything we'd ever learned about this be wrong?

21

'Mess' Gadol Haya Po

L et's back up a little bit," Rabbi Green said. The kids in the front row scooched back a bit from the sputtering and spitting oil, but I was pretty sure Rabbi Green didn't mean it that way. "First of all, my hands are a little busy at the moment. Would someone like to come up and write the letters *Nun, Gimel, Hey*, and *Shin* in Hebrew on the whiteboard?"

Many hands shot up. Hannah's arm was waving and shaking so much I was afraid it might loosen from its socket and fall right out. There's no way that Rabbi Green couldn't help but see her but he looked past her and chose someone else. If he chose Hannah every single time she raised her hand, no one else would ever get a chance.

"Dahlia, please come up and write the letters for us. Just be careful and stay far away from my desk and the skillet." Hannah dropped her arm and looked so sad you'd think her pet iguana just died or something. Meanwhile, Dahlia jumped out of her seat grinning like she'd just won a year's supply of sufganiyot, and went up to the front, keeping her distance from Rabbi Green and the spitting oil. She picked up a blue marker and, in Hebrew, wrote the letter Nun. Next, she took a green marker and wrote the letter Gimel, then an orange marker for Hey, and finally, a black marker for Shin.

Rabbi Green took a quick glance at the board and gave Dahlia a thumbs-up. "Yafeh me'od, Dahlia, very nice. *Todah*, thanks." He then motioned for her to go back to her seat.

"Now, what do these letters on the dreidel mean?" he asked while sliding the latkes around in the pan.

This time Rabbi Green pointed at Matthew.

"The letters are there so you can play the dreidel game," Matthew said. "Each player should have a bunch of something in front of them, like chocolate gelt, raisins, or pennies. At the start of the game, everyone puts one thing into the middle, which is called the 'pot.' The players take turns spinning the dreidel. If you get a Nun, you don't get anything but you don't lose anything either. Nun means nothing. Gimel is the best. If the dreidel lands on Gimel, you win everything in the pot."

Ari chimed in.

"I remember because Gimel starts with a 'G' and you 'get' everything."

"No, that's not it!" Hannah jumped in. "It's because Gimel stands for *Gadol*, which means big. So you win big!"

I couldn't help myself. I butted in on top of Hannah's jumping in. "Actually," I said, grinning at Hannah, "my grandmother told me that the letters come from German or Yiddish. The Nun stands for *Nischt* which means nothing. And the Gimel stands for *Gantse*, which means the whole thing." I was so pleased with myself for being able to one-up my main classroom competitor. She pursed her lips, and her face turned red, like a tea-kettle about to burst with steam.

Rabbi Green seemed to enjoy this little sparring

match between me and Hannah. "Okay, so this isn't what I meant when I asked about the letters. I wasn't talking about the game but rather, what the letters stand for, in terms of the history of Hanukkah. However, since we're heading down this path now, do you know what the other two letters are in Yiddish, Yoel?"

Now it was my sister's turn to jump in. She was with me when Grandma Ruth told us about the Yiddish letters.

"I know!" she said excitedly. "The Hey is for *Halb*, which means half, and the Shin is like *Stella* or something like that."

Rabbi Green gave us a big, happy smile and said, "Close! It's *Stell Ein* which means put in."

Matthew continued explaining the game from where he left off.

"As I was saying, if someone gets a Gimel, they get everything, and then each player has to put another one into the pot before the next person goes. Hey means you get half of whatever's in the pot, and if you get a Shin you have to put one in the middle."

Ari said, "You see, my system works in English too! Hey is for half, Shin is for share, Nun is for nothing, and Gimel is for get."

"Yafeh me'od! Very nice, yeladim. Now back to what the letters mean. Would someone else like to come up and write the Hebrew words *Nes Gadol Haya Sham* under each of the letters that Dahlia wrote?" Rabbi Green asked while sliding the brown, finished latkes onto the paper towel-lined tray.

All the hands shot up again. This time he chose Mia to write. As she did, he asked, "So, you see, each of the letters also stands for a word. Nun is Nes, Gimel is Gadol, Hey is Haya, and Shin is Sham. Who can tell me what the expression Nes Gadol Haya Sham means?"

Jonah said, "A great miracle happened there."

"Tov me'od, very good!" Rabbi Green replied. "And where is 'there'?"

"Israel!" some kids called out.

"Jerusalem!" others yelled.

"Nachon! Correct! Jerusalem, Israel is indeed what we mean when we say Nes Gadol Haya Sham, a great miracle happened there."

Mia interrupted. "Guess what? When we were in Israel we saw dreidels with different letters. Theirs said Nun, Gimel, Hey, Pey. The Pey stands for *Po* which means 'here'."

"That makes sense," Jenna said.

"My English version of the letters even works with the Israeli dreidels. If you get a Pey, you have to pay!" Ari announced.

Rabbi Green beamed. He loved this sort of conversation, even with all the interrupting.

"You're right," he said. "In Israel they say '*Nes Gadol Haya Po*,' A great miracle happened *here*. So, we all agree that there was a big miracle of some sort, but I still want to get back to what the biggest miracle of the story was," he said. "Now, let's talk about what was going on that led to the Temple being destroyed. First of all, who destroyed the Temple? And why?"

Ellie raised her hand to answer.

"Yes, go ahead, Yael," Rabbi Green said without taking his eyes off of the pan. He was carefully flipping a new batch of latkes, which were quickly turning golden brown and looked like they were going to have an amazing crispy crunch to them. I got a whiff of them as he turned over the last one and my mouth watered again.

Ellie began.

"The Greeks took over and wrecked the Temple, kind of like how you wrecked our room last time." Rabbi Green gave Ellie a sheepish smile.

This made me think of a joke right on the spot. Even though it wasn't my turn, I jumped in.

"I guess you could say MESS Gadol Haya Po!"

The whole class laughed, especially Rabbi Green. I love that he appreciates my sense of humor. I'm sure other teachers would have been annoyed and might have even sent me out of the room for being disruptive, but Rabbi Green enjoys having fun in the classroom as much as we do.

When the laughter died down, Ellie continued.

"Things were bad for the Jews at that time because they were being ruled by King Antiochus, who wouldn't let them, you know, be Jewish."

Know-It-All-Hannah interrupted this time.

"The Greeks even sacrificed a pig on the altar. That was the biggest insult of all. They made it unkosher!"

"Yes," Rabbi Green said, sounding pleased. "Now we're getting warmer."

She beamed once again. I spotted a few kids in the room rolling their eyes at her.

"Anyone else have any thoughts?" Rabbi Green asked. I raised my hand.

"Judah Maccabee was a Jewish leader. He and all of his followers fought the Greeks." Then I added my latest fun fact. "I recently learned that the word 'Maccabee' means hammer, so I guess Judah really pounded out the bad guys."

"Nice!" Ari put his fist out for me to give him a fistbump.

"'Nailed' it!" Ethan shouted. Then he looked around

the classroom and said, "Get it? He nailed it, because he's a hammer!" A bunch of us giggled at his pun.

"Got it!" Rabbi Green said. "So what, exactly, did the Greeks want the Jews to do?"

Guess who blurted out for the millionth time.

"They wanted the Jews to give up their religion and live like the Greeks," Hannah said. "They wanted the Jews to dress and eat like them, and even to pray to all the Greek gods."

Rabbi Green was about to start talking but Hannah kept going.

"Did you know that there was a woman named Hannah, just like me, who had seven sons—not like me?" she said, giggling a little. Then she got serious again. "She and her sons all refused to obey the Greeks' commands, and the Greeks did very terrible things to them."

Rabbi Green looked up for a second at Hannah. "Wow! How do you know all this?"

"I learned about Hannah one time when I was researching the meaning of my name," she answered.

"*Mitzuyan*, Chana! Excellent! So, for me," Rabbi Green explained while flipping the latkes, "the biggest take-away from the story of Hanukkah is that some of the Jews refused to conform. They wanted to keep their beliefs and their identity. As Chana said, the Greeks tried to force the Jews to adopt their lifestyle and to accept their gods. The Maccabees refused to go along. They fought for the freedom to pray to their one God as they wished."

I looked over at Hannah. She was glowing like a neon sign.

With each latke that Rabbi Green turned over, we heard a loud sizzle in the pan. He continued.

"This rag-tag, tiny group of untrained men was fighting a huge, well-organized, and well-equipped army because they didn't want to give up their way of life. They stood their ground and fought for what they believed."

"Yeah, the Greeks even had elephants that they rode in on. Those things could crush you like a bug," Matthew said. "Those Maccabees must have been either brave or crazy. Or both."

Goofball Ethan stood up and said, "Spoiler alert— the Maccabees won!"

Rabbi Green smiled and said, "Thanks for the heads-up, Eitan! So that, to me, is the greatest miracle in the story of Hanukkah, even more than the story of the oil. A small but mighty group of brave people worked and fought together, and managed to beat the big, giant army. Thanks to them, we're still here today."

He paused to flip the last few potato pancakes in the pan. "And speaking of miracles, my friends, today you are witnessing another miracle, right here in our classroom. Nes Gadol Haya *Po*, a great miracle happened here!"

"What do you mean?" Mia called out.

"What's the miracle?" Abby asked.

"Check it out." Rabbi Green looked right at us with a big, proud grin. "For once, I didn't burn the latkes." He held up the tray of the beautiful, brown potato goodness for us to see. "They're perfect. Now that's what I call a miracle!"

22

Double Dog Dare

Rabbi Green placed another layer of paper towel on top of the pile of latkes already sitting on the tray. He removed the last of the potato pancakes from the pan and stacked them on top of the paper towel to absorb the excess oil. They were a perfect golden brown and smelled incredible! He turned off the electric skillet, unplugged it, and looked down into the pan.

"Will you look at that?" he remarked. "I used exactly the right amount of oil. There's not a drop left in the pan."

"Another Nes Gadol Haya Po!" Dahlia exclaimed.

"Indeed, Dahlia!" Rabbi Green said. "Yafeh me'od! Nicely done." Then he added, "Excuse me, yeladim, while I return the skillet to the kitchen, where it will cool off. I'll just be a couple of minutes." He pointed with pride at the beautiful mountain of golden-fried deliciousness on the platter and said, "No touching the latkes until I get back!"

The moment Rabbi Green stepped out of the room, Ethan turned to the class and said, "I dare one of you to take a latke! Like this." He sprinted up to Rabbi Green's desk, where he took a napkin in each hand and used one to swipe the top latke from the pile. Then he ran back to his seat. The latke, fresh from the pan, was too hot to hold. He juggled it from napkin to napkin and tossed it gently over to Micah, sitting in the next seat, who immediately tossed it right back.

"Ouch!" Micah exclaimed.

"It's like playing hot potato," Sydney said.

"Well, it *is* a hot potato!" Ari pointed out.

Ethan could barely hold the latke, let alone try to eat it, so he wrapped it inside the napkins and took off his baseball cap. For a minute, I thought he was going to hide it on his head under the cap, but instead he set the latke on his desk and used the hat to hide the evidence.

"Oh, come on!" Matthew yelled. "He gave us one simple instruction, 'Don't touch the latkes'!"

"Did you even wash your hands yet? That's disgusting!" Jenna said.

"It's unsanitary, and it's also stealing!" Hannah wailed. "I'm telling Rabbi Green!"

Micah, unfazed by Hannah's threat, decided to take Ethan up on his dare. He turned to me and said, "I'm a Bravey Cat." He ran to the front of the room, grabbed a few napkins, and swiped a latke from the top of the stack. He zipped back to his seat while blowing on the latke to cool it off. Ethan motioned to give him a big high five but Micah was holding the latke with two hands. The two of them laughed like they'd just heard the greatest joke ever told.

Micah turned to me and said, "Come on, Joel, you do it. Be a Bravey Cat!" A million thoughts raced in my brain like a slideshow of all the things that had happened that week: Ethan in the bookstore, encouraging me to open the magic kit; Dad and I in the kitchen, having the discussion about not stealing; Brainy "borrowing" a nativity statue.

"Bravey Cats rule! C'mon, Coppy," he said, using my Bravey Cat name to make his point even though we were at Shul School, which violated the club's rules. "I dare you. I double dog dare you, so now you have to do it!"

"I triple dog dare you!" Ethan exclaimed gleefully.

All eyes in the classroom focused on me. My heart pounded so fiercely I could feel my blood throbbing throughout my body all the way down to my toes and up to my face, which I was sure was bright red by now. Even though I had promised not to take anything without permission, it didn't seem as bad as what Brainy had proposed with the nativity scene. I mean, one of those latkes *was* for me, right? I was getting one either way. A small part of me wanted to do it just for the thrill of sneaking without getting caught. Plus, it's really hard to turn down a friend's triple dog dare.

But Rabbi Green literally just told us not to touch the latkes.

I silently shook my head.

"Come on, Joel, it's funny! You love being funny," Ethan said. "Just do it!"

"I don't want to," I murmured, looking down at my shirt. I had made up my mind.

"C'mon, man," Micah said with a smirk, "you're the mushroom!"

I smirked too because everyone knew exactly what he was talking about. It was one of my old jokes about a mushroom that introduces itself to someone and says, "Hi, I'm a real fungi!" (But when you pronounce it, it comes out as "fun guy!")

Ethan said, "Yeah, you're a fun guy!"

Hannah jumped in.

"Actually, 'fungi' is the plural. He would really say 'Hi, I'm a real fungus.'"

"*You're* a real fungus," Micah muttered under his

breath. Ari, Ethan, and I cracked up.

Ethan wouldn't let it go. "You love pranks and jokes. Since when are you afraid of going for a laugh?"

"I don't want to. Drop it already!" I said a little louder this time.

Ari said, "He doesn't want to do it. Cut it out!"

"What's the big deal?" Micah demanded. "Watch this." He took the latke out of the napkin, waved it around to cool it off a bit and licked it. Then Ethan did the same thing.

"Stop it, that's disgusting!" Mia shouted at them.

"Why don't you leave him alone!" my sister yelled at Ethan and Micah. I appreciated her and Ari standing up for me.

"Come on, Joel," Micah urged, ignoring Ari, Mia, and Ellie. He even ran back up to the front to grab some napkins for me to use to do the job. Then Ethan started chanting, "Do it! Do it! Do it!" Micah and a few other kids joined in too. Before long, Micah was banging on his desk, and the chanting grew louder and louder. I knew only a few kids were cheering, but it felt like a full football stadium in my head. I was afraid the sixth-graders and seventh-graders were going to come running into our room like last time to see what was going on.

I sat at my seat with my arms crossed against my chest and shook my head no. I felt my face turning even hotter and redder. I didn't like everyone looking at me, and I definitely didn't like anyone coaxing me to do something once I said no. I have no problem speaking up during class and sharing my ideas, and I certainly don't mind being the center of attention when I'm putting on a magic show or telling jokes. But this was different. I didn't like being pressured in front of the whole class.

Ethan tried pulling me out of my seat by my sleeve, "Come on, do it now, before he gets back. We won't tell!"

"*I* will *definitely* tell Rabbi Green when he gets back," Hannah announced. For once, I kind of appreciated her being a tattletale. Still, I didn't want my friends to think I wasn't a Bravey Cat. At the same time, I didn't want to disobey Rabbi Green. I was mad that they were putting me in this position, and yanked my arm back.

"Stop it!" I barked at them. That's when Rabbi Green popped into the room.

"So, what did I miss? It sounded like a party in here from down the hall."

"Micah and Ethan each stole a latke from the top of the stack!" Hannah reported. "Then they licked them!"

Rabbi Green wrinkled his nose, looked at Micah and Ethan, then looked down at the floor and shook his head. "Yeladim," he said in his quiet, serious voice, "go quickly to wash your hands, then come back and form a line in front of my desk to get your latkes." We all followed his directions, surprised he didn't address the latke-stealing accusation.

As we returned to the room, he told us we could each take up to three latkes if we wanted, and if there were enough left over, we could have even more. He twisted the lid off the applesauce jar, poured some into a bowl, scooped sour cream into the second bowl, and then stuck a spoon in each.

We all lined up and waited for our turn. Rabbi Green walked over to Ethan and Micah and handed them each an empty plate.

"Eitan and Micha, you don't have to stand in line

with the rest of the kids." They looked at each other and grinned like winners of a huge jackpot. The rest of us looked at each other with faces that read *That's SO unfair!*

"I heard that you've each claimed a latke already. Is this true?" Both boys nodded, their grins melting away. There's nothing worse than being busted, especially by your favorite teacher ever, and Rabbi Green is everyone's favorite.

"Have you already eaten the latkes?" he asked. The two boys shook their heads no.

Rabbi Green continued.

"Do you remember me telling the class not to touch the latkes?" Again, they both nodded, looking down at the floor, avoiding eye contact with him. Rabbi Green shook his head in disappointment and said, "You don't need to stand in line because you've already taken your latkes, and you won't be getting any more."

The rest of us who were standing in line grinned at one another. *Yeah, okay, that's totally fair!*

Just like Dad, Rabbi Green didn't yell, but it was very clear that he was unhappy with Ethan's and Micah's decisions. We watched the scene unfold as we continued moving in our line toward the latkes and plopping sour cream or applesauce, or both, on top of them. I can't imagine anything in the world worse than disappointing Rabbi Green. Except for maybe disappointing Rabbi Green *and* not getting more latkes.

Ethan and Micah took their plates and slinked back to their seats, looking like they each wanted to crawl under the linoleum beneath their desks. I felt kind of bad for them, but then again I felt like they got what they deserved. Also, I was relieved that I had stood my ground and didn't let them bully me into stealing a latke when I really didn't want to. I would have been, as Dad says, "in hot water," just like them.

One by one we returned to our seats with our food. We were all talking and eating and having a great time.

Rabbi Green walked over to Ethan and Micah. He bent his knees and squatted down between their two desks. Although he spoke quietly to the two culprits, it was impossible not to hear him since I was only one seat away from Micah.

"Eitan and Micha, I didn't mean to embarrass either of you, but I want you to understand that we have certain rules and expectations. I specifically asked the class not to touch the latkes when I walked out of the room, and you both chose to do exactly what I asked you not to do."

The two of them sat there, looking straight down at their plates, each staring directly at his now partially eaten, sad, little, probably-cold-by-now latke.

"I'm disappointed in the choice you each made but I'm sure you'll do better next time. Enjoy your latkes and let's move on, okay?" I couldn't help but feel happy and proud of myself for not giving in to their teasing and pressure. I would have pretty much died if Rabbi Green was saying all that to me too, which of course would have been the case if I'd chosen to take on the dare.

"Sorry, Rabbi Green," Micah mumbled without looking up from his plate.

"Yeah, sorry," Ethan said.

"Thank you both for the apology. Now, let's get back to our lesson." With that, he stood up, returned to the front of the room, and announced in his ever-cheery voice, "Yeladim, while you're eating, let's talk about Hanukkah."

"Yay, Hanukkah!" some of us cheered.

"It looks like there are still a few latkes left over, so come up and get more if you'd like," he said to the class. The two latke thieves knew they were not included.

I was looking forward to the discussion and eating more latkes, but had a weird feeling in my stomach after all the latke drama. I looked over at Micah and Ethan, each slowly eating their lonely single latkes. I couldn't understand why they had bullied me like that. Micah is one of my best friends, and Ethan and I have been friends at Shul School since third grade. We never treat each other that way. Feeling a bit Judah Maccabee-ish, as a small act of defiance, I took my plate and walked to the front of the room to get an extra latke. I wasn't really hungry anymore but it made me feel better to walk past Micah and Ethan with yet another steaming-hot potato pancake. As I was sitting down, I practically stuck my whole nose into the latke on my plate, took a huge whiff, and purred like a cat, "YUM!"

I know it wasn't very nice, but it felt so satisfying, almost as satisfying as eating a delicious crispy latke with applesauce on top.

23

Who Can Retell the Things That Befell Us?

Rabbi Green leaned against the front of his desk, balancing his own plate of latkes in his left hand and happily chowing down.

While cutting into a latke with the side of his fork he announced, "Let's get back to the Maccabees and their struggle to live their lives the way they wanted. Can you imagine how much pressure they must have felt to change?" Rabbi Green wiped a little white dot of sour cream from the corner of his mouth. "Have you ever felt pressured to do something you didn't want to do?"

"Yeah, homework!" Micah called out. Apparently, he had recovered from being reprimanded by Rabbi Green. "I feel pressured by my parents and my teachers to do my homework every single night, and believe me, I never want to do it!"

Rabbi Green chuckled softly.

"My parents pressure me to shovel the driveway when it snows, and rake the leaves in the fall," Adam added.

Rabbi Green chuckled again and said, "I stand by your parents on all of the above. You should do your homework and help out at home. I'm hearing that some of you feel some pressure from the adults in your life. How about from your friends?"

A few kids nodded, including me. *Boy, have I ever!* I thought.

"Have any of you heard of the term 'peer pressure'?" Rabbi Green asked.

Jenna spoke up. "Isn't that when your friends try to make you do something you don't want to do?"

Rabbi Green nodded and said, "It is. Somebody give me an example of how your friends might try to make you do something."

Jonah said, "Well, it's not like they would force you to do something physically, but you might get teased or bullied if you don't do it."

"Or they keep on bugging you to do something until you give in and do it because you just can't take it anymore," Ellie added.

I gave a sideways glance at Ethan and Micah, who, only a few minutes earlier, tried to do that very thing to me by pushing me to steal a latke. I felt my face get red and hot all over again just thinking about it.

"Is anyone here willing to share about a time you felt pressured by your peers to do something that didn't feel right to you? Or have you ever pressured someone to do something that they didn't want to do?" Rabbi Green asked.

The room got uncomfortably quiet. Once again I gave the stink-eye to Ethan and Micah but once again they didn't seem to notice.

Finally, Adam spoke up. "I dared my little brother to put salt and pepper on his ice cream and then eat it. I just wanted to see if he'd do it. I didn't really think he would, but he did. I feel kind of bad about it now, but at the time I thought it was pretty funny."

"Oh my gosh, that's so mean," Jenna said to Adam.

"Gabe is so cute. How could you do that to him?"

"I was just joking around," Adam said defensively. "It's not like I hurt him."

"Adam, why do you think he agreed to do what you asked him to do?" Rabbi Green asked.

"I guess because he wants me to like him? Which, if you think about it, is kinda silly because I have to like him. He's my brother!"

"It sounds like he looks up to you," Rabbi Green said. "Maybe next time you can 'pressure' him to do something positive, like putting his toys away."

"Yeah," Adam answered. "I guess that would be a better idea. Maybe not as much fun, though."

Rabbi Green gave him one of his famous wink-and-smile combos.

Jonah said, "You might feel left out if all your friends are doing something, so you do it to be part of the group. Even if they don't say anything directly, you still kind of feel pressured to fit in. Know what I mean?"

Rabbi Green and a few of our classmates nodded.

"At my school, a lot of kids have been dyeing their hair funny colors," Jonah continued. "I don't really like the way it looks but I was feeling left out so I tried it. I dyed my hair bright orange using Kool-Aid powder so it wasn't permanent, thank goodness. I felt ridiculous. I looked like one of those troll dolls! I haven't done it since then but now I feel like an oddball, not going along with what everyone else is doing. Does that count as peer pressure?"

Rabbi Green nodded. "Well, I suppose if you went ahead and dyed your hair even though you didn't really want to, it could be considered peer pressure because you were conforming to something you wouldn't normally do." He put another latke on his plate and said,

"Thank you, Adam and Jonah. You each described cases when you or someone else wanted to be included and were willing to do something they wouldn't otherwise choose to do on their own. Does any of this sound a bit like the Hanukkah story?"

We sat there quietly. Some kids were busy focusing on the food in front of them, while others, like me, were trying to come up with an answer to the question. *I got it!*

I raised my hand.

"Lots of Jews during the time of King Antiochus's rule did take on the Greek way of life. Probably everyone was feeling pressure to join in. Maybe it was pressure from the Greeks and maybe it was from their fellow Jews who caved to the Greeks' pressure. That's why the Maccabees standing up for themselves was such a big deal."

"Yes, todah, Yoel," Rabbi Green said.

And then I couldn't help myself. I looked around the room, took a deep breath, and said, "I recently felt pressured by my peers."

"Do you want to tell us about it?" Rabbi Green asked.

I gave another little sideways glance at my two friends, who started squirming in their seats. Their faces turned stoplight red. They each looked over at Rabbi Green and then at me, practically begging me with their eyes not to say anything. Hannah perked up and sat at attention, looking pleased with how this drama was unfolding. The whole room held its breath.

Ethan and Micah shook their heads subtly to say, "No!" without Rabbi Green noticing. A silent debate broke out in my head.

Should I rat out my friends? Would that ruin our

friendship forever?

Maybe I shouldn't because friends don't snitch on friends. It's not like they put me or anybody in danger or anything.

But then again, they were mean to me!

On the other hand, they already got scolded for stealing the latkes.

On the other, other hand, they got in trouble for not following instructions, not for bullying me. They need to learn not to do that to anyone else ever again.

I knew I had to say something. But what? Then it came to me: *What would Judah do?*

"Well—" I started.

Everyone looked at me expectantly. Meanwhile, the two of them continued to plead with their eyes, twisting their bodies like acrobats at the circus, begging for a break. They knew that if Rabbi Green found out that they not only made bad choices for themselves but pressured me to join them as well, he probably wouldn't let them off quite as easily this time. I could practically read their minds:

PLEASE DON'T TELL HIM!

COME ON, JOEL, DON'T RAT US OUT!

I was so torn.

I hesitated for another moment, took another deep breath, looked over at my two friends, and finally said, "I'm in a challenge club at school." Ethan and Micah were so relieved that they deflated in their seats like two bike tires that each ran over a nail.

"We dare each other to try things that might be hard or difficult. We have a rule that we can't force anyone to do anything that's dangerous or hurtful, but I'm still kind of nervous about it. To be honest, I've already started to feel pressured to do things I don't want to do."

Rabbi Green looked down at the plate still in his hand. After a few seconds, he spoke.

"I do like the rule about not forcing each other to do things that don't feel right. That sounds like a very thoughtful and good rule. So, tell us more. I've never heard of a challenge club before."

"Well, we challenge each other to do different dares. The thing is, my friends have dared me to take things that don't belong to me. Another time, it wasn't actually a dare, but I felt like I was being pressured to take something that wasn't mine," I explained, thinking back to the magic kit fiasco.

Rabbi Green's eyebrows did that furrowing thing they do when he's troubled by something. He thought for a moment.

"I have to say, I was intrigued by the idea of a challenge club when you first mentioned it, but hearing the details makes me think that maybe it's not such a good idea for you and your friends." He paused and looked around the room. "Are there other students in the classroom who are in this club?"

Ari, Micah, and Ellie all raised their hands hesitantly.

"Well, the challenges aren't all bad," Micah said.

Ari jumped in. "Yeah, sometimes we do fun contests, like who can hold their breath the longest. We actually did that one. Joel almost won too," he said, looking at me like a proud parent.

"Okay," Rabbi Green said, sounding not quite convinced. "What other things might you do?"

"You know, stuff like seeing who can do the most push-ups or climb the highest," Micah offered.

"Physical challenges can be good," Rabbi Green said.

"Will you also do things like brain challenges—maybe something like trying to solve tough math problems?"

Did he say what I think he just said? It was like he was reading my mind. *I LOVE this guy!*

"We're not sure yet, but probably. At least I hope we'll do some math challenges," I said, turning toward my crew and flashing them a huge, cheesy smile. I mean, come on. If our uber-cool teacher could make such a suggestion, then maybe it wasn't such a dumb idea after all. "We totally should!"

"But we're also going to dare each other to do things to show that we're brave," Micah said. "Like watching super-scary movies or riding the scariest roller coasters. You know, stuff like that."

"Hmm," Rabbi Green said, his face still a little scrunched, like he was deep in thought. "Well, we still have a lot to cover about Hanukkah but I'd like to continue this conversation after class. Are the four of you free to stay for a few minutes today? We can let your parents know so they won't worry."

"Sorry, I can't stick around today, Rabbi," Micah said. "I have to go home, eat lunch, and then I have karate class. Sundays are always busy for me."

"Yeah, I can't stay today, either," Ari said.

Ellie and I looked at each other and shrugged. Other than having to put in my time at the bookstore, I didn't have much planned for the day.

"Joel and I can stay," Ellie offered.

"Great," Rabbi Green said with his friendly smile, "we'll continue this later."

Then, once again, almost like magic, he whipped out a bag full of dreidels and another one full of those chocolate gelt coins, and to the whole class he said, "Now, who wants to play dreidel?"

24

Be the Shamash

It's not that I was nervous about meeting with Rabbi Green, because I knew we weren't in trouble and, honestly, any extra time we get to spend with him is a bonus. Still, there's something about being asked to stay after school to talk with a teacher that makes my stomach queasy.

"Okay, perfect, I'll send them out in a few minutes," Rabbi Green said into his cell phone as he ended his call with Mom. Then he spoke directly to us. "Your mother said she's going to drive Jeremy home and come back for you, so we have a few minutes to talk."

He motioned for us to sit down at two of the desks in the front row. He pulled a third one out and turned it to face us. Now we were sitting in a sort of triangle.

"Okay, Silver twins," he started, "tell me about this club of yours."

Ellie, in her peppy way, began to tell him all about how it was me and my friends who started it, and how she, Megan, and Asha had to kind of audition to get into the club. Her eyes grew bigger and brighter as she recalled the whole scene in the lunchroom when she refused to eat the stuff that wasn't kosher. She practically bounced out of her seat when she got to the part about how Asha couldn't eat that stuff either because she observes the laws of halal.

"We were like Maccabees!" she exclaimed. "They

wanted to force us to eat some of everyone's lunch but it wouldn't have been kosher or halal. We stood up for ourselves! Joel stood up for us too, and told Brady, the leader of the group, that he can't make us do something that goes against our beliefs and our religions." She looked at me with grateful eyes and then shifted her gaze to Rabbi Green for his approval.

Rabbi Green smiled gently as he listened, and nodded his head, reminding me of a bobble-head doll.

"Yafeh! That's really nice to hear," he said to both of us. "But it sounds like that challenge put you in an uncomfortable position. Yoel, you mentioned feeling pressured to do things or take things that didn't belong to you. Tell me more about that."

I looked up at the fluorescent light above my head as I gathered my thoughts. I chose my words carefully because I didn't want to get anyone in trouble. At the same time, I did feel like I could use some help in figuring out how to deal with some of the dares my friends were coming up with.

I began by telling him about the situation with the magic kit. It wasn't a dare from the club, and I mostly made that decision on my own, but I definitely felt some pressure from my friends. Then I told him about Brady's terrible idea with the nativity scene.

I'd never seen Rabbi Green look so upset. His eyebrows bunched up and his eyes crinkled. He even frowned. I don't think I'd ever seen him frown. Ever.

"Who is this boy?" he asked. "Why do you suppose he would want to do something so disrespectful?"

I felt the need to come to Brady's defense.

"He's a kid in my class, and he's actually a nice guy. I honestly don't think he meant to do it to be mean. He said he wanted it to look like a magic trick, that the statues would disappear and then reappear. He never intended for us to actually keep them."

As I said it out loud, it sounded even more pathetic.

Rabbi Green sat and silently studied his hands, which were resting on the desk. After a few long, uncomfortable seconds, he stood up, turned away from us, and walked to the front of the room. I thought maybe he was done talking to us, that he was completely offended by us and our behavior, even though I had made it pretty clear that we didn't take that dare and that we all came down pretty hard on Brady for even suggesting it.

I watched as he bent over and opened the bottom drawer of his desk. I couldn't see what he was doing exactly, since I was on the other side. After fumbling around for a few seconds he slid the drawer shut. He returned to his seat holding something small and silver in his hand.

"Ooh, that's a pretty menorah," Ellie cooed.

"Thanks," he replied, holding it up and looking at it like he was meeting an old friend he hadn't seen in a while. "We got this one in the *shuk*, the open-air market in Jerusalem, when Rebecca and I were living there while I was in rabbinical school. It brings back a lot of memories." He paused and then asked, "Do you remember what else we call this?"

"A hanukkiyah," Ellie answered before I had a chance to say anything.

"Correct," he said. "Can you tell me why it's a hanukkiyah?"

"Because it's a special menorah for Hanukkah!" Ellie answered.

"Correct again!" he said. "Any candle holder that has multiple arms is called a candelabra in English, and a menorah in Hebrew. In fact, the word menorah could even mean a lamp in Hebrew, any kind of lamp. But a hanukkiyah, now that's something different and special. Only a hanukkiyah has nine spaces for candles."

I thought it was a little weird and off topic for him to dive into a lesson about a Hanukkah menorah right in the middle of our discussion about the Bravey Cats, but I was happy to have some bonus time with him, so I waited patiently to see where he was going.

He pointed to the single, solitary candle holder in the center of the hanukkiyah that stood above the other eight. There were four to its left and four to its right. "Now, I know you both know this. What do we call the special candle that goes right here?"

I was about to answer when Ellie jumped in ahead of me again and said, "That's the *shamash*."

"Yes," he said. He must have detected my frustration with Ellie's hogging the conversation, so he turned to me and asked, "So, Yoel, what is the job of the shamash?"

I appreciated the opportunity to participate in the discussion.

"The shamash is the helper candle. It's the one we light first, and then we use it to light all the other candles."

"Exactly." His smile grew even brighter, almost as if the menorah was lit and shining its light on his face. Then he said in a more serious tone, "I'm very proud of the two of you for standing up for what you believe is right. Yael, good job not feeling pressured to eat food that you knew wasn't right for you. Yoel, I'm glad to hear that you stood up for your sister, not to mention talking your friends out of that terrible nativity scheme."

"Thanks," we both replied at the same time.

"Now, I want each of you to be the shamash," he said.

"You want us to light the candles?" I asked. "Do you have any here?"

"No. I don't have any candles today, and I'm not asking you to light them, either," Rabbi Green said patiently. "I want you to *be* the shamash. I want you to be the leaders, to spread the light and goodness in your group. You've already started. Now I'd like to see you take it a step further."

"I'm not sure I get it," Ellie said.

"Me neither," I said.

Rabbi Green sat back down with us, looking at the hanukkiyah as he spoke.

"I would like to see the two of you be the ones to get things going in the right direction, just like the shamash does. Before we light the candles in the hanukkiyah, there's darkness. Then suddenly, a match is lit, a tiny spark in the darkness. The match lights the shamash, and then the shamash goes to work spreading that light, one candle at a time. And no matter how much light it spreads, its own light never decreases."

He paused, looked over at YaYa and said, "Yael, you look confused."

"Well, I don't really understand how to be like the candle exactly," she admitted.

"Okay, let me put it this way," he said with a smile. "You both know Mr. Pinsky, right?"

"Sure," Ellie said. "He's Jeremy's Shul School teacher. He teaches the seventh grade."

I added, "He's also always at shul walking around during Shabbat morning services. That guy never sits down!"

Rabbi Green chuckled a little. "Exactly, and can you guess why he never sits down?"

Ellie shrugged her shoulders and guessed, "Maybe he has trouble sitting still? We have some kids in our class like that."

Again, Rabbi Green chuckled and said, "Good guess, but no, Mr. Pinsky is actually the Shamash of our shul! We refer to him as the *Shammes*, which is just the Yiddish way of saying Shamash."

"So he's in charge of turning on the lights? Like the shamash lights the other candles?" I asked.

"Not quite," Rabbi Green said in his jolly voice.

Ellie and I both waited for more explanation because while I thought I understood, now I was getting more confused. Rabbi Green read our expressions and explained.

"Mr. Pinsky never sits down because he's the one who makes sure that everything goes smoothly in our service. He makes sure that people who are going to open the ark or lead a prayer know that their turn is coming up. He shows them where they need to go. He's kind of like the director. He's our Shammes, our shamash, our special helper. He sets us all in the right direction and makes sure that everyone is doing what they're supposed to be doing. And now I want the two of you to each be a shamash with your friends. Set them in the right direction and make sure they're doing the right thing, just like Mr. Pinsky does."

Ellie and I smiled because it was finally starting to make sense.

"So, getting back to you," he continued, "being in a club can be great fun. Setting up challenges for one another can be a wonderful thing, provided that the activities you propose are safe, smart, and good. I don't need to tell you that stealing and taking things that aren't yours is an astronomically poor choice."

We both nodded silently. Now we were the bobble-heads.

"I have confidence in both of you. You're already making good choices for yourselves. When I say I want you to be like the shamash, I mean that I'd like you to help guide the other kids in your group to do better. Do you see what I mean?"

We both bobble-headed again. I looked up at the whiteboard, where Rabbi Green had previously written, *What gift will you give to others that will add light on Hanukkah?* It felt like a light lit up in my head. I'd even say a menorah full of candles lit up in my head!

Rabbi Green looked down at the watch on his wrist and said, "Well, kids, I think I'd better let you go. Your mom is probably back from taking Jeremy home and waiting for you outside. When I see you in class on Wednesday, you'll let me know how it's going, okay?"

We thanked Rabbi Green, and said goodbye as we stood up and headed out into the hall.

"I think I understand what he wants us to do. Do you?" Ellie asked in a quiet voice a few steps from the classroom.

"He said he wants us to step up and help our friends make better choices. Or try, anyway. It might not be easy but he basically told us, 'Don't not try.'" I shot Ellie an impish grin after quoting Corey McDoofus.

And then she did something she never does. She threw her arms around my shoulders and hugged me. It was one of the weirdest moments we've ever had together. And strangely, one of the nicest.

25

Hanukkah Means Rededication

Word got out that I had a big idea for our club. All morning long, my Bravey Cat friends tried to pry the information out of me. One by one, they sidled up to me, hoping that I'd spill the beans.

"Come on, Coppy," Archie begged, "just tell me. I won't tell anyone else!"

"I'm dying to know about your idea. I can't wait to hear what it is," Spooner said.

Brainy even said to me, "You have to tell me. I'm in charge of the club." He punctuated this demand with a big, loud sneeze.

But no matter how many people asked, or how many times they asked, I didn't tell.

"I'll tell you at lunchtime during our meeting when we're all together," I promised. And like a great show-man, I left them wanting more. Maybe I hadn't yet mastered my most difficult magic trick, but I sure knew how to work a crowd.

When the bell rang to let us know it was time for lunch, we all hurried to the cafeteria and claimed our meeting table. We tried Salty's challenge of not step-ping on any of the lines on the floor in the lunchroom. It sounds easy but the square tiles on the floor aren't that big, so we practically had to tip-toe from one box to the next to get around the room. We looked so goofy we made ourselves laugh. That was a hard challenge but a fun one.

We settled in, munching on our sandwiches and stuff, and finally got to the heart of the meeting. "All right, Coppy, you're up," Brainy announced.

"Is your big idea that you finally came up with names for me and Asha?" Ellie asked.

Oh no! I felt terrible. I still hadn't thought of anything creative for them but I didn't want them to know. I looked around the table, scrambling for inspiration.

"Uh, yeah," I stammered, trying to act cool. "Ellie, you're going to be...Lunch Tray, and Asha, you'll be...Fish Stick!" I acted like I was super-proud of my work.

"Lunch Tray?" Ellie shouted at me. "I don't think so! That's a terrible nickname!"

Asha said, "I don't want to be Fish Stick."

"Okay, okay," I said, pretending to be hurt that they didn't like my ideas. "I'll keep working on it." Whew! At least I had bought myself some more time.

"So what was your other big idea, the one you made us wait for all morning?" Brainy asked.

Ten pairs of eyes looked at me over juice boxes, sandwiches and sticks of string cheese. I swallowed a spoonful of applesauce and cleared my throat in a long, drawn-out, dramatic display of showmanship. It got some eye-rolls.

"Okay," I started, "you know how Brainy wanted us to swipe the statues from the churchyard and return them later so it would look like they magically disappeared and then reappeared?"

Everyone nodded. A few Bravey Cats glanced menacingly at Brainy.

"I don't know what your idea is, but I can tell you

right now that I am *not* stealing anything," Spooner said in an angry voice.

"Me, neither," Asha, and then the rest of the group, echoed.

"Of course not," I assured them.

"So what's your great idea?" Tricky asked.

"Well," I continued, "believe it or not, Brainy's terrible idea—" I paused and smiled at Brainy. He narrowed his eyes at me. "—gave me the perfect idea. You know I'm totally into magic, and that I love the idea of making things disappear but not if it involves stealing."

Heads nodded in agreement—even Salty's. I guess he'd learned his own lesson about stealing at Shul School.

"I do really like the idea of sneaking in somewhere and changing things around. Maybe we can take that concept and twist it a bit."

My friends watched me with eager eyes, wondering where I was going with this.

"You may not know this, but Ellie, Salty, Archie, and I all go to Jewish religious school at our synagogue twice a week," I stated.

"You mean you have to go to more school after you go here?" Brainy asked.

"Yeah, but it's actually fun," I said, as Archie and Salty smiled and Ellie nodded in agreement.

"I go to weekend religious school at my mosque too," Asha commented. She explained that the mosque is where her family goes to learn and pray. "It's like a church or synagogue, but for people who are Muslim."

"I go to Sunday school at my church," Tricky said.

"Me too," said String Cheese.

"Anyway," I continued, "as you can guess, we've been talking a lot about Hanukkah at religious school because it begins next week. Of course, I always knew that Hanukkah was the name of the holiday but I didn't know exactly what the word 'Hanukkah' meant."

Ellie jumped in. "We just learned this week that the word Hanukkah means 'rededication.'"

"Okaaay," String Cheese remarked, stretching out the second syllable, "and what exactly does that mean?"

"It means starting all over from scratch," Ellie explained. "It comes from the story of when the Greeks destroyed the Jewish Temple in Jerusalem a long time ago. After they fought a big battle, the Jews won and were able to get back into the Temple, but it had been trashed. They needed to clean it up and start all over."

"Right, and that gave me an idea," I said. "I think we can completely re-shape this club so it's not about doing things that might be hurtful to others. Let's start all over and rededicate our club just like they did in the story of Hanukkah."

Meat lifted up one of the Crutchy Twins that was leaning against the table and said, "I wouldn't mind choosing some activities where we won't get hurt."

"Good point," Buzzy said, then turned to face me. "What'd you have in mind?"

"Brainy was on to something when he suggested doing stuff in secret and not getting caught," I continued, pleased that they seemed to be with me so far. "How about if we do nice things but completely in secret? For example, let's say there was a huge snowstorm and we met up in the neighborhood and snuck around shoveling people's driveways. The challenge would be to get it done without getting caught! People would come outside to find their driveways totally cleared and have no idea how it happened or who did it!"

"So, you mean, like, we'd still do challenges but they'd be nice? And helpful?" Buzzy asked.

"Yeah," I replied, looking around to see everyone's reactions.

"Well, I sure wouldn't want to make a habit of shoveling other people's driveways," Brainy said. "I don't even like it when I have to do my own driveway."

I could see his point.

"Maybe we'd just shovel once, after a big snowstorm. We'll come up with lots of different things to do."

"We'd be like helpful elves," Spooner exclaimed. "I love it!"

"I like it too," Tricky said. "I was kind of nervous about some of the dares we had on our list."

"Me too," Archie confessed. "I truly did not want to kiss Ms. Amato's shoes!"

What a relief to hear that I wasn't the only one who was worried about the dares.

I went on. "Our rabbi challenged us to figure out how to bring more light into the world, which is another piece of Hanukkah."

"So, we'll need to bring flashlights," Brainy said.

"Well, sure, if it's dark out, that might be helpful, but I think what Rabbi Green meant was not literally adding light, but making the world a better place. You know, symbolically adding light," I explained.

Brainy nodded as if he understood. I wasn't 100 percent convinced.

"I love this idea," Buzzy said, "but if we do it, we'd probably want to change the name of our group. Maybe we'd be, like, the Helping Heroes instead of the Bravey Cats."

"Okay," I said, "but the most important thing is that we keep it top secret. Nobody can know that we're the ones doing all this stuff. When I think of heroes, I picture them showing up to save the day with their hands on their hips, their big capes waving in the wind, and everyone looking at them in awe. We would be doing this all in the shadows, in secret."

"Instead of Helping Heroes, we could be the Hidden Heroes," Ellie suggested.

"Oh my gosh, that's awesome!" Spooner exclaimed.

"Yes!" Asha said.

"What do you think, Brainy? Are you okay with changing things up and 'rededicating' our club?" I asked.

"Yeah, I guess so, but I really wanted to take on challenges."

"We still can," Ellie said in her typically enthusiastic way. "We can challenge each other to do helpful and friendly dares. Plus, let's say we wanted to collect toys for the children's hospital or raise money for a charity. We could set a high goal and make that a challenge to ourselves that we'd have to meet."

"Yeah, okay, that's cool," Brainy said with a small nod, "but I still want to do some of the fun challenges like hanging spoons off our noses and stuff like that."

"Absolutely, of course we can still do fun stuff like that," I replied, "but for the big dares, we'll just change the focus a bit."

"Can we keep our nicknames?" Meat asked me directly since I was the nickname grand master.

"Sure," I said, "we don't have to change everything about the club—just the bad stuff."

Tricky turned to me. "Speaking of nicknames, I have ideas for Ellie and Asha. Is it okay if I make up their names?"

I wasn't crazy about sharing my one big responsibility, but in fairness, they'd been waiting a long time. "Sure, go ahead," I said.

"How about Soda Pop for you," he suggested, looking at Ellie, "because you're so bubbly and upbeat all the time."

Ellie didn't look all that thrilled.

"I don't know," she said, "I'm not sure I like Soda Pop."

"Well, you do have a sparkling personality," Spooner said. "If not Soda Pop, how about Fizzy?" she suggested.

Ellie scrunched up her nose.

"Or in keeping with this theme, how about Gassy?" I offered. Everyone at the table roared with laughter. Everyone except, of course, Ellie. She shook her fist and stuck her tongue out at me.

"Kidding!" I said, while laughing.

Then Tricky said to her, "I've got it. Let's call you Bubbles."

"Okay!" she said, full of pep, living up to her name. "That's way better than Lunch Tray or some of those other ideas." She gave me the stink-eye.

"Anything's better than Lunch Tray," said Archie bursting into laughter.

"Not Gassy," Ellie replied, smirking a little. Even she knew deep down that it was funny.

Tricky turned to Asha. "Asha, how about if we call you Champ because you keep winning all the challenges?"

Asha smiled and gave a thumbs-up to show her approval. I gave a thumbs-up too since I was in charge of the nicknames.

Brainy took over again. "Listen up, everyone. We have some things to vote on. All in favor of changing our mission to being a helping group, say 'Eyeball.'"

"Eyeball!" we declared in unison.

"And all those in favor of changing our name to Hidden Heroes, say 'Eyeball.'"

Again, we all said it.

And that's how the Bravey Cats club became "re-dedicated" as the Hidden Heroes.

26

The Hunchback of Notre Dame, Robin Hood, and the Maccabees

Did you bring the stuff?" Archie whispered to me at the entrance to the lunchroom. We were heading in for our Friday club meeting.

I unzipped my backpack and showed him the stash inside.

"Great," he said with a huge grin.

"Cover me!" I said to him as if we were playing Spy Guys, one of our favorite games to play at my house. "I have to sneak the backpack in. Ms. Amato can't see it or I'll get in trouble."

For some reason that none of us truly understands, our school has a lot of rules that don't make much sense to us. First of all, we're not allowed to wear hats in school, ever—unless, of course, you have to cover your head for religious reasons, like some people wear a kippah or a hijab. Second, we have to put our backpacks in our lockers first thing in the morning when we arrive, and we can't pull them out again until dismissal time.

"Hold on, I have an idea," Archie said as he took off his zip-up sweatshirt and put it on me, over my backpack and all.

We both laughed hysterically. "Now I look like the Hunchback of Notre Dame!"

"Just act natural," he said between giggles. "Ms. Tomato will never notice."

"Yeah, right," I said, "because I look oh so natural right now."

We came up with a better idea. Instead of trying to sneak in looking like the Hunchback of Notre Dame— out in the open—we gathered up some of our crew. String Cheese, Brainy, Spooner, Archie, and Bubbles surrounded me, covering me so I could sneak the backpack into the lunchroom unnoticed and quickly hide it under the table.

"I don't love breaking the rules," I said quietly to the group, as we shuffled together into the lunchroom as one big blob, "but I kind of feel like Robin Hood. He stole stuff from the rich and gave it to the poor. We're also doing something against the rules in order to do something good."

Bubbles added, "We're also like the Maccabees. They broke the rules because they believed they were doing something good too."

I'm sure some of the kids didn't understand what she was talking about but there was no time to explain. We had to grab our table and hide the backpack.

Our crazy plan worked. We safely made it past Ms. Amato.

Once at the table, we all settled in and swiftly gobbled down our lunches. Then we cleared off our lunch boxes and trays, and wiped down the table so it was clean and we had room to work. I passed the supplies around under the table to all of my fellow Hidden Heroes.

As we worked on our secret project, I asked the group, "What do you all think about my idea of visiting the nursing home? No one responded to my email."

I got the idea from Rabbi Green at our Wednesday class, when Ellie and I checked in with him, as promised. He said he was proud of us for changing the focus of the group to doing good things.

"You're doing *Tikkun Olam!*" he had said in his booming voice. "You're making the world a better place, one challenge at a time." I felt pride wash over me, like I was taking a shower in his words.

We talked with him about other things we could do to be helpful, even some that weren't a secret. That's when he asked if we wanted to invite the group to join him and his family to volunteer at the Davidson Residence. They were planning to go on the last day of Hanukkah, which would be the Sunday after Christmas. We liked the idea of doing something nice for old people at Hanukkah and Christmas time, especially with Rabbi Green's family. I sent an email to the group to see what they thought.

"I never check my email," Meat said, reaching for a red crayon.

Apparently, no one else bothered to check their email either, so I explained the whole thing again for everyone.

"Sure, why not?" Tricky said when I finished.

One by one, all the Hidden Heroes agreed that they liked the idea of volunteering at the nursing home too.

"How about if we didn't just help out but we put on a little show for the residents?" I came up with that idea after thinking about Rabbi Green's plan to perform his Hanukkah rap for them. "I'm already planning a little magic, juggling, and comedy act for my family's Hanukkah party, so I could do parts of it in the show. Anyone else who wants to can do something too. We don't even have to be all that talented. I mean, it's old people. They love kids!"

"Ooh, can I tap dance for them?" Buzzy asked.

"I don't know, can you tap dance?" I asked with a chuckle.

"Yes, I take lessons."

"Then, sure," I answered.

Before long, everyone was announcing what they were going to do for the show. Archie said he wanted to play piano, and Meat said he'd play guitar.

"Ooh, maybe you two can play and we can sing a Corey McDonald song," Spooner said to Archie and Meat. Bubbles nodded fiercely like her head was going to fall off.

"No!" I said firmly. "Anything but that!" And a bunch of us made gagging sounds. Then I smiled at the two of them and let them know I was kidding...sort of.

We continued working on our secret project when, all of a sudden, Salty said in a panic, "Uh oh, here comes Know-It-All-Hannah!"

Archie corrected him.

"I think you mean Needs-To-Know-It-All Hannah. She's so nosy."

Those who could, hid their supplies back under the table. I couldn't get my things out of the way fast enough, so just as Hannah walked by, I leaned over my stuff and covered it up with my body. I put my arm in front of me too, so there was no way she could see what I was working on. She slowed down when she passed our table, trying to sneak a peek.

I smiled politely and said, "Hi, Hannah," hoping she'd say hi back and keep walking. Nope.

"What are you all doing?" she asked, poking her head around.

I knew we had to handle it carefully because she

would definitely tell Ms. Amato that we were up to something, even if she didn't know what it was.

"We're working on...a surprise...for everyone in our grade," I said, scrambling for words that wouldn't give away our secret. "You'll like it, but you have to let us finish so you can get one too."

Archie jumped in, understanding what I was trying to do. "Yeah, Hannah, you're gonna love it." He gave her such a sugary-sweet smile that I thought his teeth would rot before my eyes.

"A surprise? For me too?" she asked way too loudly.

"Shhh! Yes!" I said in a loud whisper. "Don't spoil it for everyone."

"What is it?" she whispered, weaving her head around, trying to see past my body to what I was covering up.

"If we tell you, it won't be a surprise," I said, using the oldest line in the book.

"Well, when do we find out what it is?" she whispered back.

"By the end of the day," Archie promised. "And don't tell anyone there's a surprise coming."

Satisfied with this answer, she gave us a thumbs-up and continued on her way to return her tray.

"That was a close one!" Buzzy said.

As soon as the coast was clear, we all took our stuff out again and got back to work. We managed to finish just in time before the bell rang, and just as we had sneaked into the lunchroom by shuffling together as one, my posse of friends surrounded me and helped me escape without anyone noticing that I had smuggled in a backpack and smuggled it back out.

Now came the real challenge: to pull off the surprise without getting caught.

27

Secret Messages

W hat the heck?" Derek Snyder called out as he opened his locker.

"What is this?" Tamika Jones said, looking surprised and a bit hesitant as she reached into her locker to pull out the green piece of paper she had found in there.

One by one, our classmates opened their lockers at the end of the day to find our little surprise waiting for them.

Stephanie Chun read her note out loud to Marissa—or Sophie—Klein. "Stephanie, You are so friendly and nice! HH."

"Hey, mine is signed HH also," Marophie said. Then she read her note. "Mine says, 'Sophie, you make us smile every day. HH.'" *Ah, so that's Sophie!*

I watched from my locker as I pulled out a pink note from Ari that said, "Great idea, Coppy! HH."

Dylan Cooper asked out loud to anyone who'd listen, "Who's HH?"

Gregory Thomas replied, "I can't think of anyone in our grade with those initials."

From all the way down at the other end of the hallway I heard Camille exclaim, "Oh, I get it. HH means Happy Holidays!"

Archie and I looked at each other from across the hall and snickered. Only those of us in the club knew that HH stood for Hidden Heroes. But Happy Holidays made sense too.

As our classmates found the friendly notes hidden inside their lockers, the hallway filled with the roar of kids asking questions and shouting guesses, lockers clanging shut, and everyone laughing.

"But who is it from?" Dylan asked again as he turned his blue note over and over, still trying to solve the mystery.

"Yeah, who's it from?" I heard Spooner ask out loud, putting on an act so no one would suspect she was in on it.

I nudged my locker door shut with my shoulder to find Hannah's face right up next to mine. "Was this the surprise?" she asked at full volume, holding the paper between our faces. Luckily, the hallway was noisy enough that no one else could possibly have heard her.

"Shh!" I shushed her for the second time that day. "Yes, but we don't want people to know it's us. We're trying to secretly do nice things. Please don't tell anyone," I pleaded.

Her usually tense face softened, and she smiled at me. I couldn't believe it. Hannah Glick, a.k.a. Know-It-All-Hannah, a.k.a. Tattle-Tale-Teacher's-Pet-Hannah, the girl who drives me crazy, my rival and least favorite classmate, actually smiled at me.

"That was nice," she said. "Your secret is safe with me." Then, out of nowhere she added, "By the way, I know how to do the Floating Stack of Coins trick, if you ever want me to show you how."

That was so random! I found myself without words, and had so many questions. How did she know I was working on that trick? How did she know how to do it? Most curious of all, why was she being nice to me?

"You...what?" was all I could muster.

"I know how to do the Floating Stack of Coins trick," she repeated. "My cousin taught it to me last summer. It's easy, once you know the real secret."

Now I was convinced she was pulling my leg. There is nothing easy about that trick. I figured that, as usual, she must be trying to one-up me the way she does in class.

"No way!" I finally managed to say.

"It's true," she said plainly, with a little shrug. "I could show you sometime, if you'd like."

She's playing a trick on me, I thought. *Hannah would never offer to help me out with anything. And for sure, if she knew how to do the Floating Stack of Coins trick, then she was probably into magic like I was, and if so, a magician would never reveal the secret.*

"How did you know I was working on the trick?" I asked.

"I saw you trying to do it in the lunchroom," she answered. "I also saw your whole table of friends picking up all the coins that were rolling away, so I knew you were having difficulty with it."

I felt my face flush. I couldn't quite tell from the way she said it if this was the Hannah I knew from Shul School delighting in my failure, or if this was a new bizarre Hannah being nice to me and seriously offering to help me learn how to do the trick. I decided to give her the benefit of the doubt and let her know she was right, that I *was* having a hard time making it work.

"Yeah," I said with a note of sadness and frustration in my voice, "I just can't make it work."

"I could come over sometime and show you," she offered. "We magicians need to stick together."

I stood there for probably way too long staring at

her, trying to figure out her angle.

"Are you really into magic?" I asked.

"Yeah. Ever since last summer when I spent three weeks with my cousins in San Francisco. My cousin is kind of a professional magician. He does shows and performs at schools and camps and stuff. He got me hooked. So do you want me to come over and show you how it's done?"

This was by far the longest that Hannah and I had ever spoken to one another, and for sure it was the first time we talked without making faces or rolling our eyes at each other.

"Yeah...well...okay," I stammered, not sure how I felt about having Hannah come over to my house. On the other hand, I really wanted to learn how to do the trick. "That would be good," I said, stumbling over the words. "I was hoping to perform it for my whole family at our big family Hanukkah party but I won't be ready by then. Do you want to come by sometime next week when we're on winter break? That way we can work on it together so I can learn it in time to perform it at the Davidson Residence."

"Sure," she said with a nonchalant shrug of her shoulders. "I have nothing better to do."

Now that sounded more like the Hannah I've come to know!

"Anyway, thanks for the note," she said, waving the yellow piece of paper from "HH" in my face.

"What did yours say?" I asked, genuinely curious. I imagine that whichever one of us wrote it had a hard time finding something nice to say to her.

She held the paper out facing me so I could read it while she recited what it said, which she already knew by heart. "Hannah, you're so smart and you share lots of interesting facts in class! HH."

"That's nice," I said. Then just to be generous I add-ed, "It's true, you are smart."

She nodded as if to say, *Yeah, I know.* "Do you know who wrote it?" she asked.

"I don't. We took the class list and divided it up."

"Oh, okay." she said, and then abruptly started walking away. "Bye!"

"Bye," I called after her. I didn't even have the chance to ask her when she wanted to come over to teach me how to do the trick. I shook my head as I loaded up my backpack. I was pretty sure that Mom had a copy of the school directory somewhere, so I could get Hannah's number that way.

Wait! What just happened? I thought. *Who would've ever imagined that Know-It-All-Hannah would be the one to help me master my crazy-difficult magic trick? Not me, that's for sure!*

28

So Much Fire in the Living Room

As I picked off a piece of dried blue wax from my hanukkiyah, still stuck on from last year, I thought about the small silver hanukkiyah that Rabbi Green had pulled out of his drawer to show me and Ellie. He had asked us each to be the shamash, and I thought we were doing a pretty good job of it already. Our club was now "rededicated" to sneaking around doing nice things for people. We were still daring each other, but now instead of kissing Ms. Amato's' shoes or doing things like take Mr. Murphy's coffee cup, dump out the coffee, and fill it with prune juice, we were going to do things like sneak into the teachers' lounge and leave brownies. That's a serious challenge because kids are absolutely forbidden to enter the teachers' lounge. (Don't ask how we are planning to get in!) We already started strategizing how we could wash Mr. Lerman's famously filthy car in the school parking lot without anyone seeing us. *Doesn't he ever get tired of people writing "Wash me!" and drawing faces on the windows?* I have to admit, it feels so much better making plans and schemes to do nice things for others than mean ones. Plus, doing them in secret makes it even more fun and exciting.

Ellie walked into the kitchen and joined me. She reached for her hanukkiyah but it was on one of the top shelves. She tried jumping but she was way too short to reach all the way up there. I wasn't any help either, being about an inch shorter than her. Of course, when LuLu saw Ellie jumping, she needed to get in on the action. She leaped off of her back paws and barked. Her barks are so tiny, just like the rest of her, that they sound more like little yips.

Just as Ellie gave up and was about to drag one of the kitchen chairs over, Jeremy walked in.

"Ooh, Jay, perfect timing. Can you reach my menorah for me, please?" Ellie asked.

Jay has been growing nonstop since the spring. He's slightly taller than Mom now, and he's gaining on Dad. It's so crazy. I wonder if, when it's my turn to have a growth spurt like he's having, I'll end up being as tall as Jay. Or maybe I'll be even taller.

He easily reached up and, without even needing to stand on his tip-toes, pulled down Ellie's menorah. Then he got his down too.

When we were much younger, our Bubby and Zayde, who are our mom's parents down in Florida, gave each of us our own menorah to light. Originally we had one menorah for the whole family. Mom says that each of us having our own should have been a good way to keep us from fighting, but we managed to find things to bicker about anyway.

"YoYo has three red candles and I only have one!"

"How come she gets to light first?"

"Not fair! His candle is bigger than mine!"

The good news is that my brother, sister, and I don't fight about that sort of thing anymore. I mean, we still argue but at least now we don't get all caught up in dumb little fights about things like candles. I guess I do like having a brother and a sister. Most of the time, anyway.

"Kids!" Mom called down to us. She was at the top of the steps on the second floor where all our bedrooms are. "Can you please set up the little folding table in front of the window in the living room? And take down your menorahs and set them up on the table. As soon as Shabbat is over tomorrow night, we're going to light the Hanukkah candles."

"We're on it!" Jeremy called back to her. We all looked at one another and giggled because we were one step ahead of Mom for a change.

I made a fake panicked face, while still holding my hanukkiyah in my hand. "Wait! Hanukkah is tomorrow night?" As if we weren't counting down the seconds!

"Ha ha, very funny." My sister mocked me as she grabbed the aluminum foil from a drawer under the counter. "Come on, let's go set up."

Jay brought the folding card table up from the basement. He pulled the legs out from its underside and placed it right in front of the big picture window in the living room. Then we covered the table with foil and taped down all the edges. I used to think this was an official Hanukkah ritual, like, maybe a reminder of the altar in the Temple where they used to make sacrifices of grain, sheep, and other ancient stuff like that. It was only last year that I learned that we just do this so the wax won't melt onto the table and ruin it.

We placed our menorahs on the table in front of the window, which looks out onto the street. Then we each put one candle in the special place for the shamash and one candle all the way to the right side in the row of candleholders. As I passed the box of candles to YaYa, I noticed that printed on the box was the number of candles inside. There were forty-four!

"Oh! Now I get it!" I said out of the blue.

"Now you get what?" she asked, looking around, not sure what I was talking about.

"The number forty-four!" I answered.

"What do you mean? What didn't you get about the number forty-four?"

"When we were at The Silver Lining, I was reading a book called *Forty-Four Fun Facts About Hanukkah*. I didn't understand why they chose such a random number. Now I get it." I held up the candle box.

"Huh!" Ellie said.

"Wanna learn a cool math trick with that?" Jeremy asked.

"A math trick? Always!" I answered.

"Sure," Ellie added.

"Okay," he began. "Take the number of candles you need, including the shamash, on the first night and the eighth night and add them up. What do you get?"

I quickly calculated in my head. *We need two on the first night and nine on the eighth.* "Eleven," I said.

"Right. Now, add up how many you need for the second and seventh."

"Eleven again!" Ellie exclaimed.

"Now, third and sixth, and fourth and fifth."

"Oh wow! That's so cool! Did you figure that out yourself?" I asked.

"Yep," he replied.

"Wow, I'm going to have to work that into my show for Sunday! I'll make it a brain-buster question for the audience. Thanks, Jay!"

That night, we had a wonderful Shabbat dinner for the five of us. Sometimes my grandparents join us and sometimes our Aunt Rachel and Uncle David come over. Other times, we have different friends and neighbors over for Shabbat dinner, but this time it was just us. Mom had said that since she had such a busy week, and because we were going to be hosting a big Hanukkah family party on Sunday, she wanted to keep this Shabbat easy and quiet. And it was. After dinner we played many rounds of Uno and then Rummikub.

The next day, we went to synagogue in the morning and then hung out in the afternoon, reading and playing more games. Mom and Dad both took naps in the afternoon. Before we knew it, the sun was already starting to set. It sets so early in the winter!

As Shabbat was coming to an end, my siblings and I stood together by the large window in the living room, right in front of the foil-covered table. We watched the sun slowly drop down behind the trees and the roofs of the houses across the street. Our parents joined us, and together we watched the sky turn pink, then orange, then navy blue.

When it finally turned black, and all the street lights flickered on, we checked the sky to see if we could spot three stars. As soon as we did, we set up for *havdalah*, because first we'd say goodbye to Shabbat before welcoming Hanukkah. Havdalah is a short ceremony we do each week to end Shabbat and begin the new week. Ellie carried in the little silver tray with everything we needed for havdalah: a braided candle with five wicks in it, a wine cup (called a *kiddush* cup), and a spice box with tiny holes on the top so we could sniff the sweet-smelling cloves inside it, hoping to have an equally sweet week ahead.

Jewish people do a lot of candle lighting. On Friday nights we light candles to welcome in Shabbat, then on Saturday nights we light the havdalah candle to usher it out. On Hanukkah, we add one more candle each night until—by the end of the holiday—there's so much fire that our living room practically looks like the inside of the sun.

When we finished reciting all the havdalah blessings and all the singing, we each sipped some grape juice. Then came our favorite moment, when we put out the flame in whatever juice is left in the kiddush cup. We always wait to hear the sizzle when the fire and the liquid meet. It's weird but it's like a magical moment every week that separates Shabbat from all the other days of the week. Normally, that would be the end of it. We'd finish havdalah, wish each other a *shavuah tov* (a good week), and proceed with our evening. Sometimes that means going out to a movie or watching one at home, or maybe a playdate or sleepover at a friend's house. This night was different, though.

"We need to wait a minute or two before we get started with Hanukkah," Mom said. "Grandma and Grandpa want to come over and light candles with us. I invited them to stay for dinner and have latkes with us."

Grandma Ruth and Grandpa Jack are my dad's parents. They live a couple of blocks away from us, so we didn't have to wait too long for the doorbell to ring. I ran to open it, and of course, so did LuLu. Standing in the doorway were nine big boxes all wrapped in blue, white, and silver Hanukkah wrapping paper. Grandma's face peeked out from behind them. "Happy Hanukkah!" she sang out happily.

"Happy Hanukkah, Grandma!" I replied. "Can I help you with those?"

"Please!"

Jeremy and Ellie came over to greet them and each took some boxes. Our parents came to the door too.

We put the presents on the foyer floor, and everyone exchanged hugs and kisses with Grandma and Grandpa. LuLu kept doing her welcome dance at our feet while all the hugging and kissing was going on. She stopped for a second to sniff the boxes on the floor before resuming her greeting.

"Oh my goodness, look at all those presents!' Mom said to Grandma.

"Of course! I never miss a chance to spoil my grandchildren," Grandma said with a huge smile.

"Would you mind if we have the kids open your presents tomorrow night? Mark and I have a couple of things we want to give them tonight, and it might be nice to spread out the gift-giving over the course of the holiday."

"Actually," Grandma said, "we brought a gift for each of you that's special for tonight. We also brought an extra gift for each of the kids. How about if they save the second gift for tomorrow night when we come back for the family party?"

My ears perked up when I heard all this talk about presents. After our Shul School discussion with Rabbi Green about whether or not to buy presents, our family had our own discussion about the topic. We all understood Rabbi Green's message but decided to keep our minhag (or "mini-hog," as Dahlia called it), at least for this year, because we like it. It's one of our Silver family traditions.

"Okay," Mom said to Grandma. Then she said to us, "You can open the extra gifts from Grandma and Grandpa tomorrow, and we'll save the gifts from Bubby and Zayde for a different night. Looks like you're going to get a few nights of presents!"

"No complaints here," Jeremy said.

"Yeah," Ellie agreed. "I'm fine with that arrangement."

"Same here," I added.

Dad said to Grandma and Grandpa, "Here, Mom and Dad, let me take your coats."

"No, not yet," Grandma said, pulling her long, puffy coat even closer to her body. "I'm still freezing. Let me warm up."

"Yeah, me too," Grandpa said.

"As you wish," Dad said with a shrug.

We carried Grandma and Grandpa's presents to the living room and set them down.

"Okay, let's light the candles!" Dad said to everyone.

"Wait," Grandma said. "You all need to open our presents first."

"But we didn't light the candles yet," I said. "Don't we need to do that first?"

"Trust me," Grandma said, "you'll understand when you see what we brought for you."

"Who are we to argue?" Jeremy said with a laugh. "If we *have* to open presents, I guess we'll do what we have to do."

We all laughed as we passed around the six gifts with our names on them. There was even one for LuLu.

Inside each of our boxes was a Hanukkah-themed sweater. Jeremy, Ellie, and I each got one that had a hanukkiyah with all eight candles and the shamash lit. Mom and Dad got matching sweaters too. Each of theirs had a big dreidel with the letter Gimel on it.

"These are fun!" YaYa exclaimed.

"Yeah, thanks Grandma and Grandpa!" I said.

"Put them on! Put them on!" Grandma coaxed us. Then she turned to Dad and said, "I think I'm warmed up now."

"Me too," Grandpa said with a wink.

The two of them unzipped their heavy winter coats to reveal that they, too, were wearing fun Hanukkah sweaters. Theirs had two bumblebees holding shields. Below the bees were the words, "Macca-Bees."

"Ah, so cute!" YaYa exclaimed.

"We even got one for LuLu," Grandma said, pointing to the unopened package still on the floor. I opened it and showed it to LuLu. It was a blue and white doggie-sized sweater complete with a hole for the head and four holes for the legs. It had Jewish stars all around, and in the center, which would be on Lu-Lu's back when she wore it, were the words "Hanukkah Hound."

"That's awesome!" Jeremy said, cracking up.

Once we all slipped our sweaters over our heads and Dad returned from hanging Grandma and Grandpa's coats in the front hall closet, we gathered around the silver foil-covered table. Jeremy was given the job of lighting everyone's shamash. He struck a match against the side of the box and transferred the flame from the match to his helper candle. Then he took his candle and lit Ellie's shamash, then my parents' shamash, and finally, mine. So much fire in the living room, and it was only the first night! I pictured all the flames there'd be in the window on the eighth night. It would almost be like an indoor bonfire!

My brother, sister, and I sang the blessings in Hebrew, and our parents recited them in English after we sang each one.

"*Baruch atah, Adonai Eloheinu, melekh ha'olam, asher kid'shanu b'mitzvotav, v'tzivanu l'hadlik ner, shel Hanukkah.*"

"Blessed are you, God, Ruler of the universe, who has commanded us to light the Hanukkah candles."

"*Baruch atah, Adonai Eloheinu, melekh ha'olam, she'asa nissim l'avoteinu—*"

"*—v'imoteinu,*" Jeremy, YaYa, and I added together, to our parents' surprise.

"*—bayamim hahem bazman hazeh,*" we finished.

Jeremy explained to Mom and Dad, who looked a little confused.

"We just learned in Shul School that some people add 'v'imoteinu' to the blessing to make it more inclusive by honoring mothers as well as fathers."

"I'm all for that!" Mom said.

"Same!" Dad said.

"Blessed are you, God, Ruler of the universe, who performed miracles for our ancestors in those days long ago."

We sang the *shehechiyanu* last. That's the blessing we say anytime we're doing something for the first time ever, or for the first time that year. We say the shehechiyanu on the first night only to say thank you to God for letting us live to get to Hanukkah once again.

We began. "*Baruch atah, Adonai Eloheinu, melekh ha'olam—*"

Then spontaneously, the grown-ups joined in and sang the end of the prayer together with us, "*—shehechiyanu v'kiy'manu v'higiyanu lazman hazeh.*"

"Blessed are you, God, Ruler of the universe, for sustaining us and enabling us to reach this moment," Mom and Dad recited.

We each lit the one candle we had sitting alone in our menorahs. My lonely candle reminded me of a person sitting all alone on a bus with all the other seats around it empty.

Ellie must have been thinking something along the same lines because she said in a funny voice, "Don't worry little candle, starting tomorrow you'll have a friend join you and then each day you'll get more and more friends."

Jay commented smugly, "No it won't. This candle is going to melt down to nothing. This candle is gonna be gone, gone, gone. Don't give it any false hope."

Mom gave him one of her famous glares and said, "Jay!" in a tone that only she can pull off. Jeremy got the message and stopped talking.

Dad changed the subject. "Let's sing!"

And so we began to sing all the Hanukkah songs that we sing for one week each year including all two hundred verses of "Maoz Tsur," which in English is known as "Rock of Ages." (It's really only six verses but my Dad insists on singing every single one, and by the third verse it feels like it's never going to end.) Next we sang "Mi Yimalel," which means "Who Can Retell," as in who can tell the story of Hanukkah, and then "Hanukkah, Oh Hanukkah." When we sang the song "S'vivon, Sov, Sov, Sov" (which means dreidel, spin, spin, spin), the grown-ups clapped while Ellie and I spun around the room as if we were dreidels. Jeremy usually spins around the room with us, and tries to knock us over while we're spinning. I looked over at him and could tell that he was considering joining us, but, being only weeks away from his bar mitzvah, was probably thinking he was too old to play human dreidels.

"Come on, Jay, spin with us!" I called over to him. He made a big show of it, as if I had tied a rope around his waist and dragged him into the center of the living room and forced him to spin. At first, he spun around half-heartedly with his arms spread out like airplane wings. As we sang faster and faster, we spun faster and faster, and he got into it like in olden days, putting his hands together above his head, pretending to be a dreidel. LuLu, never wanting to be left out, joined right in the middle of the action, spinning around chasing her tail, barking, and jumping on us. As we spun around we got dizzier and dizzier, until we all fell in a heap on top of one another on the floor. Jeremy was right there with us, laughing and panting. LuLu climbed on the pile of us and licked all of our faces, her tail wagging furiously.

Had we ended our evening at that point, as we say at the Passover seder, *dayenu*, it would have been enough. The night was already so much fun, but then it got even better, because once we ran out of songs to sing, it was time for the best part of the night. More presents!

29

No Time Like the Present

First, Mom handed each of us kids a small, flat, wrapped gift, about the size of a book, but way flatter. It was super light, like there was nothing more than a piece of cardboard inside.

I tried to hide my disappointment because, if I'm being honest, I really had been hoping for something a little bigger. I tried not to show how I felt, but Mom must have figured it out because she said, "There will be other gifts, but I made these for you, and I'd like to start with them. Go ahead, open them up. They're all the same."

"Oh, just like Rabbi Green's family. They make presents for each other too," Ellie said.

Mom smiled as we ripped off the paper and found a plain piece of cardboard. It *was* cardboard, just as I suspected! Mom said with a chuckle, "Turn it over."

At the same time, all three of us flipped our pieces of cardboard over to find a bingo card. Of course, since Mom the artist made them, they were beautifully painted. The boards were blue with silver hanukkiyot and gold Jewish stars all around the frame. In the center was a grid with five boxes going across and five going down. Across the top boxes were five letters: G-E-L-T-O.

"Yum! I love gelato!" Jeremy said, rubbing his stomach. "Does this mean we're getting gelato?"

"What's gelato?" Ellie asked.

Mom laughed out loud. "Gelato is a type of Italian ice cream. And yes, it's delicious, and no, we don't have any gelato. Now, read it again!"

We all looked down at the cardboard in our hands. "Gelt-o," Jeremy said, "like gelt. Oh!"

"Oh. What's gelto?" Ellie inquired.

"I was trying to be creative. It's a bingo game, but for Hanukkah," Mom explained. "We're going to try to fill up the board with one thing on each of the eight nights of Hanukkah. Of course, the middle space with the gelt in it is the free space."

I read each of the boxes.

- Do something to make someone smile
- Make something special for someone else
- Eat a latke (or several!)
- Donate money to someone/a place that needs it
- Make a Hanukkah card for the people at the Davidson Residence
- Play dreidel
- Donate old toys, games, and clothes you no longer need
- Help someone without being asked

"But there are a bunch of empty spaces," I pointed out.

"Right," Mom answered. "We'll come up with the rest together."

"What if we do a whole bunch of these in one night?" YaYa asked. "Like, we're having latkes for dinner tonight and we'll probably play dreidel too."

"You only get to fill in one box per night, so choose wisely!" Mom said.

"This is cool, Mom," Jeremy said, most uncharacter-istically.

"Thanks! I thought it would be fun, and a nice way to celebrate," she said.

Then Dad asked, "Would you like to get your other presents from us tonight or would you rather wait?"

All three of us shouted at once, "Tonight!"

"Well, there's no time like...the present! Am I right, guys?" Dad said, cracking himself up. Apparently, this is where I get my corny-jokes gene from. "Okay, I'll go get them. I'll just be a minute."

We didn't have to wait long because in less than a minute he entered the living room with three gifts, all covered in blue and white Hanukkah wrapping paper.

Dad handed each of us a box of a different size.

"Should we open them at the same time?" I asked.

"How about if you open them one at a time so we can all see what you got," Grandma suggested.

"YaYa, commence the opening!" Dad announced in a broadcaster-style voice. "We'll go in alphabetical or-der, so Ellie, Jeremy, Joel."

Ellie wasted no time. Before Dad even got around to saying my name, she tore the paper off to find a plain brown cardboard box. No hint of where it was from or what it was. She opened the box, removed all the tissue paper, and let out a blood-curdling scream like she was in a horror movie being attacked by zom-bies. It startled us all. Grandma literally jumped out of her seat. Then we realized that it was a scream of joy. Surprise, surprise. Inside the box was a Corey McDon-ald T-shirt, his new CD, and the biography she had hugged at The Silver Lining.

"Oh my goodness! It's perfect! How did you know?" We all laughed. Anyone who knows my sister is well aware of her Corey McDonald obsession. Even our grandparents, who aren't familiar with his music, know about YaYa's Corey-crush. She'd only been talking nonstop about the book and CD for the past century.

"Thank you so much!" she gushed. She ran over and hugged our parents, and wiped a few tears from her eyes. Then she sat down with the CD and studied the names of the songs on the back.

Jeremy opened his box to find a small envelope buried in a lot of tissue paper. He eyed the envelope curiously, and then opened it up.

"Sweet," he exclaimed, "this is awesome!" He held up two tickets to one of the NCAA Final Four basketball games. That's practically the finals in college basketball. "I heard it was going to be here this year. This is amazing! Thanks, Mom and Dad!"

I was about to open my box when my sister shrieked, "Oh! My! Goodness! No way! No way! No way!"

"What's going on?" Dad asked, looking a bit concerned.

"Is everything okay, sweetheart?" Grandma asked.

"Okay?" my sister asked incredulously. "It's better than okay! There's a Hanukkah song on this album!" she shrieked. "I can't believe it. Corey is absolutely the most perfect person in the world. I thought I couldn't love him any more, but I was wrong!"

"That's cool," I said about the Hanukkah song, surprising even myself. "What's it called?"

"'My Heart is Melting Like a Red Hanukkah Candle'! I could just die!" she said, wiping away a few more tears of joy.

"Yeah, me too," Jeremy said sarcastically. "Listening to his music makes me want to curl up and die."

"Catchy title," I said, with all the snark I could muster.

Jeremy snickered and gave me a fist bump.

So far, my parents were hitting home runs with their gifts. I wouldn't have minded tickets to the basketball game too, but I guess they had something else in mind for me. I wondered if I'd love my gift as much as Jay and YaYa were loving theirs. I lifted my box onto my lap. The size and weight felt suspiciously familiar but I couldn't be sure.

I pulled the dreidel and menorah wrapping paper off, and couldn't believe what I was looking at. At first I thought it was a Mr. Melvin Magnifico Magic Kit. Then I saw that it looked similar because it was from the same company. But this was a brand new, unopened, still in-the-plastic Jim Junior's Genuine Jumbo Giggly-Jiggly Juggling Kit.

I looked up at my parents with awe and a great deal of surprise. I didn't even know that such a thing existed.

"Deluxe edition!" Mom said with a proud smile.

"Wow! This is amazing!" I exclaimed. "I'm going to be a master juggler!"

Dad said, "Well, I hope you'll also keep up your magic skills. You've been doing such a great job at the store that we've sold quite a few Melvin sets since you started performing."

"Time out! You've sold a bunch of the magic kits?" I asked, astonished to hear this breaking news tossed off so casually. "Why didn't you tell me?"

"I wanted to surprise you. In fact, we sold so many that I had to order more. That's when I discovered that they also make a juggling kit. You've more than paid off what you owed for opening the kit, but I do hope you'll continue to come in once in a while to perform, even after the holiday rush is over."

At that moment he reached under the couch and pulled out the Mr. Melvin Magic kit from the store that I'd been using for my performances. "I know you've been bringing the book home. Now you can hold on to the whole kit and bring it with you to the store when you perform."

I was speechless. I couldn't believe this was really happening. I walked over to Jeremy and said, "Pinch me."

He punched me.

"I said pinch!" but it was the proof I needed that this wasn't a dream.

"I can't believe this!" I said, rubbing my now sore shoulder. "I get this awesome juggling kit *and* I can hold on to the Melvin kit? Are you saying I can keep this one too?"

"Sort of, but not exactly," Dad explained. "You can use it at home but it really belongs to the store. If I ever need to put one out on display, or if you're going to perform, this is the one we'll use. I can't sell it at this point but there's no sense keeping it in the back room collecting dust. Hold on to it, enjoy it, and keep working on your tricks. Think of it as a loan rather than a gift."

This was too good to be true. "Oh wow! Thanks so much, Dad! Thanks, Mom!" I ran over and hugged both of them.

"I'd love to see you do some magic," Grandpa said. "How about if you put on a little show for us tonight?"

"Yeah! I'd love that! I can juggle too. It will be good practice for tomorrow night's party." I turned to Mom and Dad and asked, "Is that okay?"

Other than Jay, my whole family seemed to be into it, but especially Grandma and Grandpa.

Ellie turned to me and said, "Maybe you'll get so

good at magic that someday you'll be able to make Corey McDonald appear in our living room and do a spectacular concert for us!"

"YaYa, not even the greatest magician in the world could get that guy to do a spectacular concert." I said dryly.

She socked me playfully in the arm. "Very funny."

Great, now both arms hurt.

I looked over at the table with all the candles burning, and noticed that they had melted down to tiny stubs already. Unlike Shabbat candles, Hanukkah candles don't last very long. I guess all the singing, the spinning like dreidels, and opening the presents took up a bunch of time.

Dad noticed too.

"Looks like the candles are almost burned out already. Who's ready for some latkes?"

"And applesauce!" Mom added. Finally, her big moment had arrived. We were already getting kind of tired of all the applesauce, but we couldn't wait to slather it on top of those delicious latkes.

We waited in the living room until the candles finished burning and melting. My parents say it's not safe to leave the candles unattended, so we all knew that we wouldn't go to the dining table until the last one went out. The colorful wax from each candle dripped slowly and formed beautiful, colorful puddles on the hanukkiyot and the foil that covered the table.

When the last candle finally went out and let off a wisp of smoke, we headed straight to the kitchen to put dinner on the table. "Hey, everybody, want to know how many latkes I could eat?" I asked.

In unison they all said, "How many?"

"A whole lat-ke!" I answered.

30

Abra-candelabra!

A plate stacked high with Dad's blue-sprinkled Hanukkah cookies tempted us from the kitchen counter. Jay tried to sneak one.

"No way, dude!" Dad said, laughing. "Those are for after dinner."

"Oh, man!" Jeremy pretended to be very sad.

"Something tells me that those cookies are going to disappear, and it won't be one of my magic tricks," I quipped.

Since Grandma and Grandpa were joining us, we couldn't all fit at our kitchen table, where we usually eat dinner, so we all sat down together in the dining room. We enjoyed our delicious dinner of salmon, roasted veggies, and of course, latkes and applesauce.

And yes, we all ate a *lat-ke*!

When we were done, Dad carried the plate of cookies to the table, careful to not let any fall off.

"*Now* you may have some cookies."

He placed the plate in the center of the table, and my brother, sister, and I all pounced on it like lions attacking a zebra on the savanna. The first one I got was shaped like a menorah. The second one was a Jewish star. The third was a dreidel. As I reached for a fourth cookie, shaped like a Maccabee shield, Dad said, "Hey, hey, kids, slow down! I made enough to last us through the holiday. Pace yourselves!"

"Dad," I said with a sly grin. "You know how one of the miracles of Hanukkah is that there was only enough oil to last for one day but it lasted for eight? In our house, it will truly be a miracle if the cookies you made for eight nights will last for even one." I was pleased that everyone in the room laughed. I made a mental note to use that joke in my show.

YaYa asked our parents, "Are we going to have sufganiyot?"

Mom answered, "I bought some that you can have in the morning with your breakfast. They're over there." She pointed at a big, white bakery box tied with a red string sitting on the kitchen counter, right by the refrigerator. I would know that box anywhere. It was from the best bakery in the world, called Thompson Treats, which happens to be right down the street from The Silver Lining.

Man, I love Hanukkah! Donuts for breakfast? That's pretty much unheard of in our house, except for this one time each year.

"So, how about that magic show we were promised?" Grandpa asked. I love that he really wanted to see me do my stuff and wasn't just saying it to be polite.

"Oh, yeah," I replied. "Let me go set up a couple of things, and I'll be ready for you in a few minutes. You all stay in here and I'll let you know when to come in."

I ran to the living room and got all my supplies. I opened up the Melvin Magnifico Magic kit, put on the cape and the hat, and took out the magic wand. Since my show was going to be Hanukkah-themed, I chose Hanukkah props. I was going to juggle some Hanukkah candles, so I took three from the box that was sitting there: a red, a blue, and a green one. I placed them all on the table. I put some chocolate gelt coins on the table too. I decided to use those when performing the coin trick like I did in the store, instead of real coins. The biggest challenge was to make sure they didn't get squished in people's pockets. That would be a huge mess!

I wanted to do a vanishing act but still had to figure out what to make disappear. I paced around the room, looking high and low, racking my brain, trying to think of just the right thing to use.

Hmm. What could I make disappear? Not the hanukkiyot. Definitely not the unopened presents. My siblings would never forgive me if I made their presents go away.

Finally, I got it: a sufganiyah! I snuck into the kitchen, silently untied the red string, opened the Thompson Treats box and took a peek. There were different varieties of donuts inside. I decided to go with a plain jelly donut that didn't have powdered sugar on it so it wouldn't be too messy. I slid it onto a paper plate, closed up the box, and re-tied the string. I grabbed another paper plate and returned to the living room. Fortunately, nobody saw me.

I removed all the hanukkiyot from the table and placed them on the window sill. Next, I put a long tablecloth on top of the foil that was taped to the top of the table. The tablecloth reached all the way down to the floor. I placed the sufganiyah on the paper plate, which I covered with a special box from the Melvin kit. The box is like a cube but instead of having six sides, it only has four—on the front, two sides, and top. The bottom is open and so is the back. The top of the box has a hole to stick your finger into so you can lift the box and show what's inside without giving away that there's no back to it. I put the extra plate on the floor directly behind the table.

Here's how the trick works: I would lift the box to show the audience the sufganiyah sitting on the plate on the table. Then, once I'd covered the sufganiyah with the box, I'd quickly slide the sufganiyah off the plate through the open back. With a little luck it would fall onto the plate below and not onto the floor. No one would be able to see any of this because the table-cloth would cover anything going on under and behind the table.

Once everything was in place, I called my family to come join me in the living room. My heart beat a little faster as showtime approached. They were an eager audience, though, which is always very helpful. Well, almost everyone was eager. My brother kept trying to sit on a folding chair to my left, rather than in front of me like everyone else. The Vanishing Sufganiyah trick would only work if he couldn't see me swipe the donut from the box onto the plate on the floor. He was being such a pain in the you-know-what. He refused to move.

"Jeremy," I said in my sweetest, sappiest voice, "would you please join the rest of the audience in the viewing gallery?" I was already playing my role of Joel the Incredible.

"The what?" he asked obnoxiously.

"The viewing gallery," I said, trying to remain calm and patient. "Please join the rest of the audience in the area reserved for guests." I gestured to the area in front of the table where everyone else was sitting. I was try-ing so hard to stay in character. In reality, I was ready to bop him.

"Guest!" he cried out incredulously. "I live here, I'm

not a stinkin' guest!" He was having way too much fun tormenting me.

Finally, I couldn't help myself. I broke character and whined, "Mom! Jeremy's ruining my show!"

"Am not," he retorted, crossing his arms and sinking even deeper into the chair. "I just want to sit here. I'm comfortable."

Mom shot him one of her laser beam glares and said, "Jeremy Aaron Silver—"

Ooh, he was in for it now. You know it's game over when your parents resort to using your middle name.

"Move. Now." She was using her I-mean-business voice. "Joel is waiting for you so he can put on his show. Stop being a troublemaker and come sit with us." He didn't budge.

As soon as Mom called Jeremy a troublemaker, I knew exactly what Dad was going to say next. Right on cue: "Jeremy, you remind me so much of Aunt Rachel right now. As we always say, she's 'nothing but trouble.' Behave yourself!" Dad gave us all a friendly wink. He ribs Aunt Rachel like that all the time. She's my dad's sister and she is, in fact, known to be the family prankster and troublemaker.

Mom was losing her patience. "Jeremy, let's go. Move over, please."

"Fine!" Jeremy huffed as he picked up his chair and slammed it down two inches over.

"More," Mom said, getting angry.

He growled and grumbled something under his breath that we couldn't hear, and moved the chair over, closer to the group.

"Thank you," I said in a cheery voice, as if he had just offered me a piece of apple pie. I was back in magician mode and ready to perform.

"Thank you," Mom repeated quietly to him. He sat with his legs out in front of him, arms crossed against his chest, and slumped into his seat. For the life of me, I don't know why he was being so difficult, other than that's how he often behaves.

I started the show by launching into some good Hanukkah schtick.

"Oh no! Where's the gelt? I seem to have lost the gelt I was going to use for a game of dreidel. Do any of you have it by any chance?" I asked my audience.

Before long, each and every one of my family members found a gold foil-wrapped chocolate coin in their pocket or purse, depending on where I was able to set it up ahead of time. I loved seeing how surprised they were. That trick earned me plenty of applause, and everyone enjoyed their chocolates.

I did pretty well juggling the Hanukkah candles but I did break the green one at the very end. I learned that I would need to grab them more gently in the future. Or maybe I'd try juggling whole boxes. That might be easier. I still got lots of applause for the juggling. It made me even more eager to dive into my new Jim Junior juggling set.

"Hey, YoYo," Ellie chimed in, "maybe for your Hanukkah show you can try juggling dreidels."

"Or latkes!" Grandma added, laughing.

When Grandma said that, my brain immediately zipped back to that day in Shul School when Ethan and Micah stole the hot latkes and had to juggle them from hand to hand because they were so hot.

"I actually saw that once!" I said.

Grandpa said with a chuckle, "You could try that! And you know what would be even more impressive? If you juggled handfuls of applesauce and sour cream with it!" He cracked himself up with his own joke. His white mustache bobbed up and down as he shook with laughter at the thought of it. I guess bad jokes run through all three generations of my family.

"Hmm, I'll think about it," I said, joking back. I tried to picture myself doing that trick. Even in my imagination it didn't end well.

The Floating Stack of Coins trick would have been the perfect one to do with gelt, but I still hadn't mastered it yet. I was looking forward to learning the technique from Hannah. In the meantime, I moved on to the biggest act of my show: the Vanishing Sufganiyah.

I stuck my finger through the hole in the top of the box and lifted it, showing the audience the donut without them seeing the open back of the box. Next, I swiftly replaced the cover and sneakily slid the donut onto the plate on the floor. No one noticed, thanks to the long tablecloth.

I waved my magic wand over the box and uttered, "Abra-Candelabra." I got a lot of blank, confused stares. I explained, "A candelabra is called a menorah in Hebrew. Get it? So instead of Abra-cadabra, it's Abra-candelabra!" My parents and grandparents laughed, my siblings, not so much. I lifted the box.

"Voila!" I sang out. "It's gone!" Everyone seemed genuinely impressed. Even Jeremy. I stepped in front of the table and I took a long, deep bow. They all applauded for a long time, and I didn't stop them.

"Now can you bring it back?" Ellie asked once the applause died down.

I hadn't been planning on it but knew what I had to do to make it happen. I'd have to distract them, make them look somewhere else so I could quickly squat down, pick up the donut, and put it back on the plate on the table.

"Sure I can!" I said, as if I'd done it a million times. Then I "accidentally" kicked one of my juggling balls across the living room. "Oops!" I cried out. "Can someone please grab that for me? That wasn't supposed to happen."

As planned, everyone looked at the ball rolling along the floor. Dad bent over to pick it up. Quick as lightning, I reached down to get the donut, but to my horror, it wasn't there!

31

Innocent Until Proven G-E-L-T-Y

Jeremy!" I bellowed. "Why did you do that?"

"What?" he asked, acting all innocent. "I didn't touch your ball."

I was furious. "I'm not talking about the ball! You know what I'm talking about!"

He was putting on a pretty good act. If I hadn't been so mad at him I might have been impressed with his excellent acting abilities. He truly looked dumbfounded.

"No, I have no idea what you're talking about," he said, growing angry.

I screamed at the top of my lungs, "Give me back my donut!" I had no doubt that my freckles were completely camouflaged by my bright red face. A tear streamed down my very hot cheek.

Now my brother's face started turning red. "I don't have your donut!"

"Did you *eat* it?" I was beyond furious. I felt like I was going to burst.

He walked over to me and whispered, "Is this a part of your act?"

"No!" I screamed right in his face. "I know you took it!"

He backed away from me, growing angrier and angrier by the second.

"Why are you accusing me? I've been sitting here

the whole time just like everyone else. How could I have possibly taken it? Don't you think you would have seen me eat it?"

"You've been trying to mess up my show this whole time. Why are you doing this?" Another tear rolled down my face.

"Kids, please stop arguing," Mom pleaded. "We'll help you look for the donut, YoYo." She got down on her hands and knees and started looking around the table. Dad, Grandma, and Grandpa all got up from their seats and looked under their chairs. Maybe they thought since the gelt magically appeared at their seats, so might the sufganiyah.

Ellie came over to me and said, trying to cheer me up, "Well, you really did make it disappear. You're a better magician than you even knew!"

"Oh no!" Mom said from the floor.

"What's wrong? What's going on?" Dad asked.

Mom lifted the long tablecloth and out popped Lu-Lu, prancing and dancing with her furry face covered in crumbs and red jelly.

"I think we've found the sufganiyah thief!" Mom exclaimed.

"Aha!" Grandpa called out. "Caught you red-handed!"

"I think you mean red-snouted!" Ellie said with a laugh. "Or red-pawed!"

I, too, let out a relieved laugh as I wiped away the last tear.

"Ladies and gentlemen, my assistant LuLu!" I announced, trying a little humor to break the tension in the room. It worked too. Everyone but Jeremy laughed. But even Jeremy, who was definitely still mad, couldn't help but smile when he saw LuLu, the guilty culprit, jumping around with her tail wagging,

"She seems fine," Mom said, "but Mark, could you please call the vet and make sure we don't need to bring her in? Good thing I didn't buy chocolate donuts."

I wasn't too worried about LuLu. Chocolate can be bad for dogs but I'd never heard anything about jelly donuts. While I wasn't too worried about LuLu, I did feel bad that I had accused Jeremy of something he didn't do. Clearly, he wasn't over it. He had skulked away into the kitchen. I followed him.

"Leave me alone!" he snarled with his back to me. "I'm so mad at you. Why would you assume that I did that? I'm not an evil monster, you know."

"I know," I said quietly. "I'm really sorry. I just got the impression from the way you wouldn't move your chair earlier that you really wanted to ruin my show. I'm not sure why but that's how it seemed. I'm very sorry that I wrongly accused you. Please forgive me."

He turned around and stared at me for a few seconds, then asked, "Haven't you ever heard of someone being innocent until proven guilty?"

I couldn't help myself. I had to make a joke.

"Gelty," I murmured.

"Huh?" he asked, annoyed and confused.

"It's Hanukkah. You're innocent until proven *gelty!*"

My joke did the trick and broke the tension. Jeremy let out a little throaty noise and tried to hide it, but I definitely caught the corners of his mouth curling up into a tiny smile.

I repeated my apology. "I'm very sorry. I shouldn't have assumed that you did it."

He stared at me a little while longer and finally said, "Fine. I accept your apology. But I wasn't trying to ruin your show. I just wanted to see how you did the tricks."

As I stared right back at him, an idea popped into my brain that I was pretty sure would smooth things over with him. *I can't believe I'm about to do this,* I thought to myself.

"I'll tell you what," I offered. "If you want to learn, I'll teach you some of my tricks, but only if you promise to keep them top secret."

"For real?" he asked, genuinely surprised that I was being nice to him, just like how I couldn't believe it when Hannah was being nice to me.

"Yes. But you really have to promise that you won't share the secrets with anyone." He nodded. *"Anyone!"* I added for emphasis.

"I promise," he said, cheering up.

"Okay, then, I'm going to tell you how to do the Vanishing Sufganiyah trick, the version that doesn't involve our pet stealing it." We both laughed. Then I did what I never thought I'd do. I revealed the secret to him.

"That's so cool!" he said. "Thanks for sharing that with me. Want to go back and try it again?"

"I do!" I sneaked another donut and hid it behind my back as we rejoined the rest of the group in the living room.

Everyone was fawning over LuLu. Dad got off the phone and told us that the doctor said she should be okay but we should keep an eye on her. While they were all huddled together paying attention to LuLu, I set up the trick again. I invited everyone to sit back down for a repeat performance of the Vanishing Sufganiyah.

They all resumed their positions but this time,

Mom held LuLu in her lap. LuLu seemed to be fine, but she had calmed down considerably since her grand entrance from under the table. She wasn't her usual spunky self. Her tail still wagged, just a bit slower.

Once again, I did all my schtick and made the donut disappear from the box. This time, just as I was about to make the donut reappear, Jeremy jumped up from his spot and cried out, "Ouch! I think I got a splinter from the wood on this chair!" It was just enough of a distraction for me to put the donut back while everyone was crowding around him, examining his finger. All agreed there was nothing there, and they all sat back down.

"Abra-candelabra-which-is-menorah-in-Hebrew!" I recited as I waved my wand. I then lifted the box, and the donut was once again on the plate. The audience was wowed, and I secretly gave Jeremy a thumbs up for his Academy Award-winning performance.

In a million years, I would never have guessed that I would share one of my magic secrets with someone, much less that I'd share it with my rotten, evil, older brother! (Okay, okay, he's not really all that bad, I guess.) Not only that, but in that same million years, I would never have guessed that he'd actually want to help me with my magic act, not just mock me and make fun of me. It was a Hanukkah miracle! Nes Gadol Haya Po! A Great Miracle Happened Here, in our living room!

My audience demanded an encore, so I did a few of my favorite card tricks. Even Jeremy participated. He even laughed at my jokes! As I shuffled the deck, I threw one out there:

"Hey, why don't the animals in the jungle ever play poker?"

"I don't know, why?" Jeremy asked, the loudest of everyone.

"Because of all the *cheetahs!*"

That got a few laughs.

We had a lot of fun until it was time for Grandma and Grandpa to go home. LuLu perked up enough to follow Grandma and Grandpa to the foyer to say good-bye, and gave each of them a parting lick on the hand. Once they left, the house got pretty quiet.

YaYa and Jay and I sat down on the floor to fill in our G-E-L-T-O boards. We each made a big X on the spot that said "Eat a latke" as well as the free space in the center. I knew I'd be able to fill out the "Make someone smile" box at my next performance at the family party, or else at the Davidson Residence, so I left that one open. Some of the other boxes would be easy to fill in, like "Play dreidel" or "Help someone without being asked," and some would take a little more effort. Either way, I was sure I'd be able to get "bingo." I mean "G-E-L-T-O."

Hanukkah was off to quite a start. And to think, we still had another seven nights to go!

Acknowledgments

In a Latke Trouble has been a roller coaster for me to write. Sometimes the ideas flowed so quickly that I could barely write them down fast enough—my fingers on the keyboard couldn't catch up with the ideas pouring out of my brain. Then at other times, I was so stuck, the ideas wouldn't come and I didn't even try to write for weeks. In the end, it all came together, but just as it is with any other major project, I couldn't have done it without the help of so many people.

I would like to thank:

My kids:

Ilana, the original Bravey Cat: You un-stuck me! I was so frustrated with the story and couldn't figure out exactly how to put all the pieces together. You and your index cards and your creative ways at looking at things got me out from under that big metaphorical rock and got things rolling again. Thank you for being you and for being my kid! Ari and Eitan: You were the very first ones to read my manuscript and to give me feedback. Even though you don't live at home anymore and even though these books were once appropriate for your reading level, I love that you are still so involved in this work that I do. Forrest, one of my honorary kids: I appreciate all the time we got to spend together this year, and I want to thank you for jumping right in as a first-round reader.

Gary: As always, you've supported, encouraged, and coaxed me on with my writing. Thank you for all of your technical and editorial expertise as well as your commentary and input. I couldn't do this without you!

To my very own group of Bravey Cats—the kids

who read my very first manuscript and shared their thoughts and ideas. Thank you so much for all of your help. I hope you enjoyed the process as much as I enjoyed working with you! My Bravey Cats: Akiva "MonkeyMan" O., Aliza "Princess Intelligent" O., Cassie "Book Sloth" B., Corban K., Ellie "Potato" W., Gavi "Incrediboy" G., Izzy "Wise Girl" M., Kane "Hurricane" M., Lisa "LiLi" I., Maddy "Monkey" S., "Mermaid" Maya F., Noah "Noshki" Z., Otto "Obscure Otter" O., Sam "Samurai" S., Stephanie "Stevo City" P., Yaara "Yaya" W.

My editor Leslie Martin: I can't begin to tell you how much I enjoy working with you. I can't understand how it is that when we spend time, wordsmithing, dissecting and rebuilding sentences, debating the use of certain terms, we look at the clock and see that two hours have flown by! Working with you is so much fun and so rewarding. I'm already looking forward to the next book with you. Thank you for your wisdom, kindness, and patience with me and all my exclamation marks!!!!

The adults who also read my manuscript and provided me with invaluable feedback, constructive criticism, and insights: Rabbi Avi Olitzky, Melanie Heuiser Hill, Jennifer Wilson Coats, Amy Robbins, and Lisa Simon, Thank you all so much for being a part of this experience! Thank you also, Rabbi Alexander Davis, who not only gave me feedback, but also wrote up questions for a discussion guide which will be available on my website. (www.yayayoyo.com)

I would also like to acknowledge that, while most of the information and facts about Hanukkah came from my own life experiences, I did use two online articles that I found while researching for this book. The first article, "The Surprising Origin of the Dreidel" by Rabbi David Golinkin, can be found on the My Jewish Learning website. (www.myjewishlearning.com/article /the-origin-of-the-dreidel/)

The second article, "The Real Reason American Jews Give Gifts During Hanukkah," by Rabbi Menachem Creditor can be found online at *Time* magazine. (www.time.com/5747552/hanukkah-gifts-history/) Interestingly, after referring to this article, I met Rabbi Creditor, first online and later in person due to our worlds happily colliding. Rabbi Creditor graciously offered to read my manuscript and offer his kind words for a blurb about the book. I love our small Jewish world! Thank you, Rabbi Creditor, for being a part of this book, both knowingly and unknowingly!

Ann Koffsky: You did it again! I love the cover of this book and how you always bring YaYa and YoYo to life with your brilliant artwork and vibrant colors. Thank you so much!

Yaffa Cohen Appelbaum: Thank you for teaching me about sfenj! Now I'm looking forward to coming over to your kitchen this winter to taste it. Also, you get all the credit for coming up with the term "*Mess Gadol Haya Po*." That's one of my favorite additions to this book.

Stacy Pinck Birnberg: Thank you for giving me permission to use your idea to destroy a classroom in order to teach about Hanukkah. I remember when you did this in your second-grade classroom and what a powerful lesson it was. You are an amazing, creative teacher and a wonderful person in general!

And finally, I would like to thank the readers of the YaYa & YoYo books for your continued support. Thank you for all of your wonderful letters and emails, and for being in touch with me on social media. You are the reason I do what I do! I am now beginning to brainstorm ideas for Book 5 about Tu B'shvat and the environment. Stay tuned!

Sliding Into the New Year

(Book 1)

Thrill-loving fifth grader Ellie Silver (YaYa) has been waiting all summer to visit the brand new indoor water park in town. She is ecstatic when her best friend, Megan, invites her to go—that is until her twin brother, Joel (YoYo), points out that Megan is going on Rosh Hashanah. Sure, Rosh Hashanah is a big deal, but so is Splash World! What will Ellie do?

Shaking in the Shack
(Book 2)

Joel Silver (YoYo) loves to be a comedian and to play practical jokes. However, when he, his twin sister Ellie (YaYa) and the rest of their fifth-grade Hebrew School class find something surprising in the synagogue's sukkah just before the holiday of Sukkot, it's no laughing matter. Where did the mysterious four-legged visitor come from? What will become of it? Their unexpected adventure brings Joel and Ellie face to face with the importance of shelter and caring for those in need.

Hoopla Under the Huppah
(Book 3)

Ellie Silver (YaYa) doesn't think she believes in super-stition. Yet it seems like lately everywhere she goes and everything she touches brings bad luck. She thinks she may have even upset something called the Ayin Hara, also known as "The Evil Eye." Ellie has been counting down the minutes until she, her twin brother Joel (YoYo), and older brother Jeremy will be in their favor-ite aunt's wedding. But with all the unfortunate events leading up to the wedding, Ellie wonders if it will just be one gigantic disaster. And how much of that will be her fault? She needs to figure out how to get rid of the bad luck—and fast!

About the Author

Dori Weinstein is an award-winning author who grew up in Queens, New York. She is a graduate of Binghamton University (SUNY Binghamton) and Teachers College, Columbia University. Dori has taught in schools in New York City, Minneapolis, and St. Paul, Minnesota. When she's not creating new adventures for YaYa and YoYo, Dori enjoys visiting schools around the country, both in person and virtually, where she teaches about Jewish books, writing, and publishing. Dori lives in Minneapolis with her husband Gary. They have three grown children, who have flown the nest and are out in the world creating their own adventures.

Visit Dori on Facebook, Twitter, Instagram, and on her website at www.yayayoyo.com.

Made in USA - Kendallville, IN
73813_9780989019330
11.30.2022 1327